MADE TO BE
Mastered

MADE TO BE

Managing Your Emotions Successfully -- God's Way

Jon Tal Murphree

Baker Book House
Grand Rapids, Michigan 49506

ISBN: 0-8010-6169-5

Printed in the United States of America

To
my students and former students
at
Toccoa Falls College
who have given me the kind of education
every professor needs

Contents

Introduction

According to Ludwig Feuerbach, man is the creator of God in his own image. But then Feuerbach is left with no explanation for man in God's image—no adequate accounting for all the godlike qualities in man.

The proposition of God as Creator is not a blind assumption of the Christian system; but that argument can be found in other books. In these pages I will presuppose the idea of God as Creator (regardless of what creative method HE may have used).[1] Rather than attempting to prove God's existence, I wish to show how man psychologically needs God's existence.

Therapists who attempt to counsel patients purely within the social dimension are short on essential tools —which is not to say all counseling requirements relate directly to God. This book offers no spiritual cure-all. But there are some basic, underlying needs that, unmet, can render a person unable to cope with the pressures of life. These needs are spiritual in nature, and have to do with

---

[1] While I personally subscribe to the concept of direct creation of human life, the thesis of this book will accommodate other notions of creation just as well—so long as God is held as ultimate intentional creator.

one's relationship with God as Creator, and they are a common thread running through the entire human race.

Human beings possess godlike attributes that approximate the divine (in kind, not in scope)—a capacity for unselfish love and rational thought, an appreciation of beauty, the desire for truth, the inclination toward moral goodness (despite the disinclination), the aspiration for meaningful fellowship with God. The distance between nonlife and the lowest forms of life may be smaller than the distance between other creatures and humans. Indeed, human emotions require an appropriate relationship with God for their fulfillment.

This volume falls under the general category of psychology of religion, and more specifically under psychology of Christian experience. I have attempted to relate the theological to the psychological, and vice versa, by investigating the psychological implications of the Christian doctrine of man—specifically man as a created individual. This includes both the fact that he is created and the kind of person he has been created to be.

While this book may be considered psychological, I have avoided as much as possible the use of technical language—psychological, theological and philosophical —attempting to present something both digestible and nutritious for the layperson in these fields.

Jon Tal Murphree

1

The Higher-Programmed Life

It was the longest trip of Luther Bridgers' life, though it lasted for only a few hours. The terrifying loneliness that burned in his heart was made even more tormenting by the monotonous roar of train wheels on the track beneath him.

The traveling clergyman was on his way from Middlesboro, Kentucky, back to what had been his home in the Bluegrass. This time, however, there would be no family to meet him. The day before his home had burned to the ground, and his wife and two daughters had died in the fire. The train trip seemed like a journey through dark, empty space.

Earlier, Bridgers had written the words and melody to a popular gospel hymn that had brought blessing to many lives. Now circumstances made the hymn message ironic, almost absurd. Surely Luther Bridgers' mind retraced the words of his hymn as the train followed the winding track through the eastern Kentucky mountains:

> There's within my heart a melody,
>   Jesus whispers sweet and low:
> Fear not, I am with thee, peace be still
>   In all of life's ebb and flow.

> Feasting on the riches of His grace,
> Resting 'neath His sheltering wing,
> Always looking on His smiling face,
> That is why I shout and sing.

The following day Bridgers stood in the funeral parlor before three caskets, his neighbor standing at his side. Feeling the need to make conversation, the friend inquired, "Bridgers, do you remember your song about the music in your life? What about the music now?"

It was a cruel question, unthinkably cruel, but it was a question that needs to be asked. Is all the talk about divine help in troubling times just that—only talk? Is it merely something nice for the minister to say from the pulpit and for the congregation to sing about? Or can the music remain in the soul when life is disharmonious?

Before answering his neighbor's question, Luther Bridgers paused a long moment to be sure he gave an accurate answer. Finally he replied, "If I know my heart, the music is resounding deep in my soul just as melodiously this moment as it ever has in my life."

This story reads like fiction, but it has been told without exaggeration. And Bridgers' answer has been repeated over and again by many with similar heartaches.

Short-circuiting Tragedy

Given life's absurdities and ludicrous contradictions, the question is this: Is there any *reasonable* way tragedy can be short-circuited before it deals a devastating blow to the human personality?

When we are the victims of trouble, we can react with complaints, criticism, and self-pity. This may temporarily make the trouble easier to handle, but the critical attitude we develop in the process becomes more damaging than the trouble itself. Or we may anesthetize ourselves by becoming resigned and stoical, but this, too, is a form of evasion and may cause more problems than it solves. We might even attempt to "utilize" the trouble, preparing ourselves for future trouble. This does give us a purpose to latch onto, but the purpose seems unworthy of the sacrifice required. It seems unreasonable.

To be reasonable, a purpose must be discovered that is so far beyond the trouble that the trouble is diminished. It need not be a purpose *for* the trouble, as if God had arbitrarily imposed the trouble to accomplish His purpose. More therapeutic is to find a purpose *beyond* the trouble—a purpose in life that is all-encompassing. This will absorb the contradictions to which there are no solutions; it will be a sort of master program that will ultimately dissolve the ambiguities—without requiring an answer.

If earthly experience by definition includes the inexplicable and the ambiguous, obviously such a purpose must be found in a dimension beyond earthly experience. This is not to suggest an other-worldly escape from the present world, but rather an acknowledgment of a larger dimension than life on earth. In order to function at its very best, the physical needs the metaphysical, the human needs the divine, the earthly system with its limitations of time and space needs the spiritual system above and beyond those limitations. Without such higher purpose, we mortals simply have no program for living that is sufficient to tie together life's frayed and tattered edges.

The Psychological Need to Have Been Created

Psychologically, we *need* to have been created. We require purpose. And there is no way we can discover that purpose if life is pure chance.[1]

To be created means there is a purpose behind my life that is greater than any purpose I might generate for myself. When I appropriate the purpose *behind* my life for my greatest purpose *in* life, I have something to bank on when my fortunes are lowest. In other words, when I have nothing to live for, I still have everything.

Divine purpose is required not only for life to be intelligible but for the human personality to have the necessary framework for facing life's cruelest and toughest incidents. This higher purpose is prerequisite for coping intelligently with tragedy. When lower-programmed life can see nothing more than futility, the higher-programmed life sees purpose and meaning sufficient to sustain the human spirit—in a way that makes sense over seemingly senseless turn of events. Rather than being an escape *from* the human predicament, this is a way to find adequate resources *within* the predicament.

In a way I hesitate to say these things, for my personal exposure to tragedy has been limited, especially when I consider those who have walked in Luther Bridgers' shoes. I can say, however, that my awareness of divine purpose in my life has been a stabilizing force in what

[1]Whether our emotional need-to-be-created points to a Creator is another matter. To some of us it definitely does so, though the evidence for God-Creator only begins here.

trouble I have known. Bridgers, however, did experience life's greatest reverses, and in the worst he could still sing:

> Though sometimes He leads through waters deep,
> Trials fall across the way,
> Though sometimes the path seems rough and steep,
> See His footprints all the way

And thousands like Luther Bridgers have kept the music during life's most difficult moments because they were plugged into resources beyond themselves.

The Preventive Ingredient

From what I have said one might infer that the higher-programmed life is primarily for emergencies. God then is little more than a spare tire and faith is little more than a shock absorber to cushion the road surface of life. In this view, the higher purpose is available as a patch when the lower purposes become threadbare. The larger system of life is seen as an emotional hideout for those ill, aged and unfortunate persons who need a retreat. Many have picked up the idea that God is little more than a celestial broadcaster who pipes heavenly music into one's life when the world is harsh with discord.

Strangely enough, this is precisely the attitude many have about vitamins, nutritious food and adequate rest. Rather than necessary to sustain health, they are perceived as useful only in restoring health—curative rather than preventive. As long as I have my health, many would say, thanks, but I'll enjoy my gluttony and overindulgence.

Though health may continue for a period without its necessary ingredients, rest and nutrition and a measure of temperance are essentials for physical life. Without necessary vitamins and minerals, we become unable to fight infection. In the same way, our lives may go on for awhile without the higher purpose, but then we become anemic and emotionally impoverished. We must discover that God is not primarily a medicine to combat poor emotional health but a necessary ingredient to sustain good health. We are emotionally structured for the higher-programmed life when we are not in trouble as well as when we are. When everything in life is going our way, we still require the higher purpose to be emotionally fulfilled.

Luther Bridgers handled his misfortune with strength because he had built into his life the esssentials of emotional health. He did not have to "appropriate" God for the tragic circumstance—he already had God. His basic emotional needs were met in advance. He had a happy life in the good times and a happy life in the bad.

2
Divine Accessibility

The great Swiss psychologist Carl Jung is reported to have said to a patient, "You are suffering from loss of faith in God." The patient inquired, "But Dr. Jung, do you believe the doctrine of God is true?" To which the famed doctor replied, "That is no business of mine. I am a doctor, not a priest. I can only tell you that if you recover your faith, you will get well. If you do not, you will not."

Most of us could not generate a personal faith against our better judgment, regardless of how much we might need that faith; pragmatism is no final test of truth. But our minds are made for truth, and our minds operate best inside this structure. The highest truth our minds can confirm is precisely what our lives require. Real truth can be tested conceptually and pragmatically—confirmed by our minds and required by our lives.

It is hardly deniable that the Christian faith offers what man needs in his personality; the gospel is utilitarian in its effect. In a culture saturated with secular entertainment, in a society requiring constant striving for economic survival, with a million other things to pull us away from God, the human personality keeps drifting back toward God. Significantly, almost twice as many

Americans attend public worship each week as attend
major league football, baseball and basketball games in
an entire year.

Made for God

Some would argue, however, that Christianity merely
developed historically to meet the needs and emotional
desires of humankind, with no necessary reference to
truth at all. But the practical effectiveness of faith can
just as easily show that God made man to need the God
who does exist. The other evidence we have for God
loads the scales to mean this.

Without much analysis it is easy to assume that
gasoline is made for automobiles. My car will not run
without it, so I can conclude the whole purpose of
gasoline is to be found in the need of my car. The
existence of gasoline is justified only in terms of what my
car requires to back out of my drive and take me to my
office.

A closer look at the internal-combustion engine, however, shows me something quite the opposite. The notion
of gasoline is logically prior to the concept of gasoline
engine. The engine was originally created to function in a
way consistent with the nature of gasoline. The combustion engine was made in full knowledge that combusti-
bility was reality. Combustion was not made for the
engine; the engine was made for combustion. In order to
burn, gasoline does not need a car. But in order to
function, a car does require gasoline. The one can do its
thing totally independent of the second. The other is
completely dependent on the first to do its thing at all.

The concept of God has not been developed to meet
the needs of man; rather man has been made in such a
way as to need God. The presence of God is the moving

power for the engines of our lives. Divine power does not need us; you and I require that divine Presence.

In the last chapter we talked about how the fact that we are created individuals gives us purpose. But we not only need this divine send-off; we need daily divine accessibility. I need access to the Source of my existence today, and this gives more than purpose—it gives personality Presence.

Here's the way it works on the human level. My son and my daughter need, among other things, two special things from me. First they need to know they were wanted, that they are not considered outside intruders by the family, that I wanted them to be my children. This gives them the basic security they need on the human level. (An adoptive parent can meet this need as well as or better than a biological parent, because no parent ever adopted a child without wanting the child. It was his purpose to do so.)

Second, my children need my *presence* as a father day by day. They need me *to have been* their father, but even more they need me *to be* their father. They need me not only to have chosen them but also to relate with them.

The Divine Presence

My children are now becoming old enough to realize that God as the source of their existence had a purpose behind their lives, and that He is available as a living Presence for their lives each day. This Presence will remain for their personality fulfillment after their dad is long gone. The wholeness and security they felt as children on the human level in the home will continue to be experienced on a higher level.

It is not that our lives function best by faith whether there is a God or not. Rather it is because there is a God behind our lives that our lives operate best in daily conjunction with God. You see, God's highest purpose in creating us is for us to experience His Presence. As much as we need the purpose behind life, it becomes more solid and tangible when it is found in the living Presence. We have been created *by* God with the built-in capacity *for* God—created with the purpose of interacting with divine Personality-Presence.

Without it, we are living life apart from the purpose of creation and are therefore living life against itself. Having been made for the ultimate we are forced to settle for the immediate. Made for the eternal we settle for the temporal. Made for God, we have to settle for ourselves; but because we are not made for ourselves we make boring company. Created to be at home with God, without God I can never really be at home with myself.

Before I was married, I once asked my younger brother who had been married several years how it felt to be a married person. He said he felt as if "it was intended for my wife and me to be together," so much so that he would get to feeling lost when he wasn't with her. When you're with your spouse, he said, you just feel at home anywhere in the world. Now I can say precisely the same thing about my own marriage.

I knew Christ before I knew my wife, and I felt at home with God long before I felt at home with her. His presence is my emotional nest. I am away from home without Him; with Him I am at home—anywhere in the world. I need this. I could not live without it.

3
Emotional Dependence

The weather was turbulent and the clouds around our plane were choppy like ocean waves. Sitting behind me was a young woman who kept shouting profanities and obscenities every time the small craft hit an air pocket—until everyone around her was thoroughly disgusted. Finally the weather became so violent that it felt as if our commuter plane was being tossed all over the sky. Suddenly the frightened young woman began praying aloud, "Oh God, save us; don't let us crash!"

A few minutes earlier she was flaunting her independence by cursing God. Now she was totally dependent and was praying.

Jesus told a parable about a young man who sought independence from his father. He was granted the independence and his life became one merry pleasure-chase—until his money was spent and he became hungry. Back to his father he came for groceries. He discovered that his independence was illusionary and temporary; it was only a dream. Survival required dependence on an outside source, on a source higher than himself.

We often see young men who want to be independent from their dads, but who want their dads to provide everything they need for their independence. It is their drive toward independence that exposes their basic dependence.

This contradictory attitude is very much a part of the average human. We want to be independent from God—we do not want to feel responsible to God, and certainly not accountable. But we want God to provide us with air to breathe, a mind to think and a body to enjoy living in. This is not independence; this is dependence.

Our emotional dependence on God is pointedly illustrated by our physical dependence on Him. From our physical limitations we should understand the feeling of dependence that is necessary for emotional and spiritual fulfillment.

In a *Peanuts* comic strip, Charles M. Schulz has Lucy saying, "It's my life, and I'll do whatever I want with it. I'm my own person! It's my life, and I'm the one who has to live it!" In the last frame she grins and adds, "With a little help."

So God Is a Crutch?

But in our self-centeredness we brandish our supposed independence for the world to see, unwilling to admit even to ourselves our own inadequacy. It stabs our egotism and punctures our pride. Somewhere we bought that big sophisticated lie that God is a crutch for those who cannot stand alone. So we attempt to bulldoze independently through life, holding our heads arrogantly high, refusing to let anyone know we need God.

One way or another, however, reality will put up a roadblock. Like Lucy, we discover we are inadequate for our own lives and in need of outside help. Standing alone we can never make it.

Does a lame man refuse to use a crutch simply because it is a crutch? Have you ever heard an amputee complaining about the sheer existence of crutches? For those who need it, the crutch is something to be appreciated, not something to be ridiculed and belittled.

Take me for example. I am physical, I am social and I am spiritual. Being a physical creature, I need food, water, air, exercise and rest. But I do not consider these things crutches. Nor do I become so independent that I refuse to breathe. Physically I am a dependent person.

Being a social creature, I need the fellowship of other persons. As a man, I need woman. I am both emotionally and physically incomplete and unfulfilled within myself. But I do not belittle myself for needing my wife. Neither do I consider my wife a crutch. Rather she is my own fulfillment and completion. Alone, I am never adequate for my social needs. But do I belittle myself for being social and needing you? And should I consider you a crutch?

In much the same way I am a spiritual being. I am made for air, for the opposite sex, for fellowship with other persons, *and* for God. Without fellowship with Him, I am incomplete. My spirit becomes starved. I become emotionally deprived. Without even knowing it I begin to develop all kinds of mechanisms to compensate for my unused religious inclinations.

If you wish to call God a crutch, then, the word has to be defined in its positive sense. In that case, you could consider our need for God something like spiritual lameness. Attempting to hobble through life without God reminds me of a lame man who has thrown away his crutch. He would prefer to crawl on his hands and knees than to depend on a crutch and stand upright.

The person who tries to live without God is like a four-year-old child who packs his bag, sneaks out the back door and starts out to make a go of it alone in the world, independent of his parents. Or he is like a high school dropout who is sure he already knows everything he needs to know.

Substitute Props

A person may stagger through life for awhile without God, propped up by his wealth, his health, his drive and determination. But these are crutches, too. He is depending on all the things God has given him instead of on God Himself. But these substitutes are false security props that sooner or later will collapse.

The actor Dean Jones reports, "I was making as much as fifteen thousand dollars a week. I was married to a lovely lady who loved me. As far as the world was concerned, I was a success . . . But I knew that life must have something more."[1]

Those who have everything—wealth, fame, power, pleasure, fortune—eventually become disillusioned with it. By the thousands they have realized, "It does not satisfy!" Some of the wealthiest men in the world have also been some of the most miserable. Whatever credentials we may have in life, we have been made for more than this world can deliver. In that same interview, Dean Jones explains how he has zeroed in on God and found that "something more."

In the chapters that follow we shall look more specifically at the particular areas of life that require God for

---

[1]Quoted by Dennis Washburn, "Dean Jones: Born Again," *The Birmingham [Ala.] News*, 5 March 1978, section E, p. 1.

emotional fulfillment. Here I will mention only one area of this dependency.

Cosmic Misfits

So far as we know, man is the only creature who concerns himself with ultimate reality. If any animals have capacity for rational thought, it stops at the point of ultimate abstract values. The rational capacity of man, however, seems to be categorically different from that of the animals, rather than simply greater. In his most reflective moments man has always concerned himself with "that beyond which there is nothing." The notion of ultimateness is so fixed in our curiosity that we cannot shake it loose.

This is not all. For centuries man has been carrying around an almost presumptuously daring suspicion that he can in some way relate to the ultimate. He even has the feeling that he "was intended" for the ultimate, that he has been made for more than things temporal and relative.

The idea of ultimate reality is a mental notion. As soon as we get the idea that we can relate to the ultimate, however, the emotions become involved. When the mind asserts, "I was made for the ultimate," the emotions respond, "If I do not relate to the ultimate, something is wrong." Emotional frustration, uneasiness, and discontent follow.

We get the feeling that we are cosmic misfits, unworthy of the kind of universe for which we are made, dropouts somewhere along the road of becoming. We feel out of native habitat, confined to and suffocated by the immediate when our spirits are native to the ultimate. Homelessly we wander on, feeling estranged from our authentic personhood.

Because our minds are programmed to entertain the notion of ultimateness, our emotions are equipped to rest at ease within the context of the ultimate. There we can let our weight down, and our restive spirits reside in tranquillity.

For this kind of at-homeness for our spirits in a relative, temporal and limited world, we are emotionally dependent on God.

4
Loneliness

The loneliest people are not those who are alone. If you want to find lonely people—I mean *really* lonely people—go to the high-rise apartment complexes in the great metropolitan centers. You will find those who are not acquainted with their neighbors living on the other side of thin walls. You will find widows in storefront apartments in rundown sections of the city who see through their windows hundreds of passers-by each hour, not one of them stopping to speak.

The emotional pain of intense loneliness today grips millions of Americans. It has become epidemic in our society. Many suicides are attributed to overwhelming loneliness, but most of them take place in cities with thousands and even millions of people all around. How can a person be lonely in the midst of so many people?

Man, a Social Creature

Loneliness is not necessarily aloneness. There is a big difference between being alone and being lonely. Consequently you can be alone without being lonely, and you can be lonely without being alone.

Loneliness has its basic source in the feeling of not belonging, not being wanted, not being included. This feeling of not being accepted can be more acute in a crowd than in solitude, so the pain of loneliness may be most severe with many people around. It is often in the presence of others that one feels unaccepted, misunderstood, and not a part of any meaningful relationship.

A lonely person is one who does not know God and who finds himself alone among believers at a prayer meeting. A lonely person is a teenager secluded in his own room, listening to popular records with a repetitious lament of broken relationships.

In the Genesis story God said, "It is not good for man to be alone." Psychologists and sociologists agree that human beings are social creatures, but it takes the philosopher-theologian to explain *why* man is by nature so social. The answer sounds simple—God made man that way.

Created as a social being, no person within himself is complete. Not only do we have a desire for other persons —we have a deep emotional need for others. Thus there is within us a basic insufficiency when we are excluded from the fellowship of other persons. Built into our emotional structure is a fundamental lack, an emotional gap, a basic inadequacy. I need you, and I hope you need me. Without others there is a certain emptiness in life.

One reason many persons feel more complete in a bar than in a church is that they feel group acceptance in the bar. There, they belong. Part of it, to be sure, is that they refuse to allow themselves feelings of belonging with the church group. They allow themselves to be accepted in the bar more than in the church. But regardless, they do happen to find a niche for themselves in the bar that mitigates their loneliness. They belong to the group.

A Paradox of Creation

If God created man inadequate to fulfill his own emotional needs, did He leave us with no solution? Do we suppose God was distracted from His plan before He saw it through to completion? Did God tire of the project and turn us out nine-tenths finished? Is the creative evolutionist to believe the process will not be complete until we each become a self-contained and self-sufficient unit, not needing other persons at all?

Hardly. Rather, we see here a paradox of creation. My own incompleteness is one of your most valued possessions, and your incompleteness has great value to me. You see, I need to feel important to someone, and I could not be important to you in the least unless you needed me. If I were sufficient for myself, I would not need you. But because I cannot assuage my own loneliness, you meet a need in me that I cannot meet myself. You become important to me. When I provide the social fellowship that you need, I become important to you. By building within us a need for one another, God has made us important to each other. In so doing He has allowed your inadequacy to fulfill one of my greatest needs—the need to be needed. What a beautiful arrangement!

Now if you feel emotional isolation, the obvious thing to do is to take the initiative. Reach out toward others; don't wait for them to reach out to you. When some may not respond, it is no cause to feel severe exclusion or rejection—there are always some who will respond. The ones you need are the ones who need you.

A lonely woman complained to me that the sophisticated class up the street did not include her in their social activities. I asked about the lower class down the street who would have taken great pleasure in her friendship. She replied, "Oh, I would not be seen in their company. The society ladies would never accept me." She wanted the group that did not need her and refused her fellowship to those who did need her. She lived on that street as a lonely individual, and died on that street without friends.

We can be so selective that we fail to meet the needs of those who need us—and then there will be no one around to meet our needs. When we are lonely for friendship, we must look for those who are lonely for friendship. We must be willing to meet their needs, and we must be willing to allow them to meet our needs—in a way that comes most easily for them.

Then something happens that is very meaningful. The moment two persons share their loneliness, they cease to be lonely at the point where they are sharing. Loneliness cannot be shared and remain loneliness. To the extent the loneliness is shared, to that very extent it is no longer loneliness.

Spiritual Loneliness

So far I have talked about only one kind of loneliness— social, or human, loneliness. There is a much deeper kind that is often overlooked by psychotherapists, a loneliness that cuts through to one's personality center. The philosophers call it existential loneliness, but we can call it spiritual loneliness.

Why should a young man in his mid-thirties travel several hundred miles just to talk with me? Ronnie hardly knew me. His wife had left him, taking his children; he was estranged from his parents; he was in trouble with the law; he had attempted suicide. Certainly he had unbearable human loneliness. But he had many friends closer by who could help eliminate that human pain better than I.

A clergyman has very little to offer in any area other than one's relationship with God. But two classes of people keep coming to us ministers for help—those who have everything and those who have nothing. One group has no need of anything material and the other knows we have nothing material to give them. But both groups keep coming.

Every Ronnie is not estranged from his family and in trouble with the law, but every Ronnie has the same basic need for God.

We humans have not only been created as social beings, we have been made as spiritual creatures. As social creatures we need one another, but as spiritual beings we need God. We have been made that way. Having both a social and a spiritual nature, we have spiritual needs as well as social needs. Within ourselves we are both socially and spiritually incomplete. Now both of these personality inadequacies can severely affect a person emotionally. Both social and spiritual fulfillment are therefore emotionally therapeutic, while loneliness in either area can result in emotional devastation.

After Jan became a Christian she was disappointed to discover she still needed friends. Knowing God did not make her invulnerable to human loneliness. She became "complete" in Christ (Col. 2:10), but she was still socially incomplete.

What her fellowship with God did do for Jan, however, was simply astonishing even in the area of her social needs. Overcoming the existential loneliness met such deep emotional needs that it prevented the human loneliness from becoming emotionally obsessive. The burning intensity of social isolation was diffused. When she did not feel the understanding support of friends, she felt the understanding and acceptance of God. When she was isolated from others, the divine fellowship was closer than the air she breathed. She gained a security in the universe that gave emotional stability in the world. Then she was in a position to reach out with acceptance toward others. Having God as a friend made it easier for Jan to make human friends. The spiritual helped resolve the social.

For Terry the situation was quite different. He did not need God, so he thought, because he had his friends. He did not feel the intensity of spiritual loneliness as long as he could duck back into his human friendships. But he did not dare allow himself to be alone for long periods of time, for the overwhelming sense of aloneness in the universe would become almost unbearable. Companionship with friends could dispel his human loneliness, but it could never drive away his loneliness for God.

Alienated from the Transcendent

This existential loneliness is basically the feeling of not belonging to anything or anyone beyond the social group. It is a sense of alienation from anything transcendent or ultimate, a feeling of isolation from real meaning or true purpose beyond the immediate. It is a sense of isolation from above-human fellowship. This spiritual loneliness is often hazy and cloudy like emotional smog, never clearly defined by the mind. But there is an underlying uneasiness, often a feeling of frightening uncertainty about one's direction and destiny in life. It all results from being unattached from the God for whom we have been made.

While having been built for human fellowship, we

have nevertheless been overbuilt than mere human fellowship. We are made with a capacity for divine occupancy. The God-shaped vacuum within our spirits can only accommodate the Spirit of God. Made for God, our spirits are forever empty and unfulfilled without Him. Made for fellowship with Him, we can never be ultimately satisfied with any lesser fellowship.

We all have inner secrets so deeply embedded in our spirits that we are unable to share them with any earthling, though we may try for a lifetime. We actually live on a deeper level than the level on which we are able to share. We need a Spirit that is able to penetrate our spirits. In our aloneness without this Spirit, we can become unbearably lonely. Deep inside, our spirits keep crying out, "I was made for God; give me God." Attempting to satisfy this spiritual need with social fellowship alone is like feeding our souls peanuts.

Much of the complexity of the human spirit is reducible to one simple maxim: Having been made for God, man is not adequate for himself. He is not self-sufficient; he is incomplete. He is never his biggest and best self until he is in fellowship with God.

The lack of acceptance man feels with God comes not from any rejection on God's part. Rather, it comes from man's unwillingness *to accept God's acceptance* of him. This sounds like a riddle, but it is not. God has not walked out on us; we have walked out on Him, thus detaching ourselves from His acceptance and isolating ourselves from God's emotional support. God has not shut off His fellowship—we have shut it out. It all began when we first recognized our separate and individual existence and began to assert ourselves against God. Sin has driven a wedge between us and God. Not made for this kind of separation, we have not been able to handle the loneliness that followed.

The result of this disruption has been two-fold. First, it has caused the sharp pain of existential loneliness.

Second, when we violated our relationship with God, we turned inward on ourselves, becoming narcissistic and self-centered. We also became competitive and defensive. This seriously impaired our relationships with one another. Sin not only had the primary effect of existential loneliness, but it had the secondary effect of human loneliness. Our separation from God has created a self-centered competitiveness that has resulted in separation from our fellow man. The result is a deep spiritual loneliness for God and a social loneliness for other persons.

When Jesus died on the cross, He took my loneliness on Himself. My sins that had separated me from God then separated Christ from God. His loneliness in that hour was both social and spiritual, feeling as if He were forsaken both by man and by God. My self-centeredness would not let Him belong to me, and my sins could not let Him belong to God.

Yet in His own separation from God, Jesus overcame my separation from God. By identifying with me, He reconnected the broken relationship and reconciled me to God. My loneliness for God is dispelled; He has become an intimate friend.

With God's fellowship, any human loneliness I may experience becomes less frustrating. My basic emotional need for friendship beyond myself is fulfilled, and I become less dependent on human fellowship. Human lonelines loses its sharpest sting.

In his *Saint Joan*, George Bernard Shaw has Joan of Arc saying, "Do you think you can frighten me by telling me that I am alone? . . . It is better to be alone with God— His friendship will not fail me."

For more than thirty years Mother Teresa of India has

lived with those unloved and unwanted human beings in the slums of Calcutta, bringing the compassion of Christ to the diseased and dying who have otherwise been forsaken and forgotten. Known as the missionary to the dying, she has spent her life with the dispossessed and downtrodden, inhaling the stench of filth, touching diseased bodies, holding dying slum-dwellers in her arms. Yet almost constantly Mother Teresa wears on her face a bright warm smile.

At the age of eighteen she left Yugoslavia to become a Christian worker. "When I was leaving home," she has said, "my mother told me something beautiful and very strange: 'You go, put your hand in Jesus' hand, and walk alone with him.' "[1] She placed her hand in that hand that has a nail-scar, and with Him she has walked alone for fifty years. Yet never for one minute has Mother Teresa been alone.

We have all been made for this divine companionship. Though we at times feel alone in the world, with Him we are never alone.

[1]Religious News Service report, quoted in *The United Methodist Reporter*, 19 May 1978, p. 3.

5
The Identity Crisis

Who is Leon Spinks? The name has been around quite awhile; most sports-minded persons recognize it immediately. Until dethroned when Muhammad Ali won the title for the third time, Spinks was the world heavyweight boxing champ.

Recently Spinks said, "People were always asking, after I won the title, 'Who is Leon Spinks?'" Then he added, "It's a question I've been asking all my life. I didn't know who I was but I knew I wanted to be somebody . . . I was tired of being a nobody."[1]

"Identity crisis" has become a well-known phrase in recent years. "Searching for my self-identity" has become popular talk in certain social circles. Some behavioral scientists keep reminding us that we have lost our authentic self-image and we therefore do not know who we are.

Quite frankly, I am tempted to be offended when I am told I do not know who I am. I reply, "I'm Jon Tal Murphree; that's who I am." But I must admit that when

---

[1]Bill Lyon, Knight-Ridder News Service report, quoted in *The Birmingham [Ala.] News*, 1 October 1978, p. 2-C.

I have said that, I have not said a lot. For Jon Tal Murphree within himself is hardly worth identifying. If someone asks, "Who is Jon Tal Murphree?" I reply, "That's me." So I have identified myself with my name and I have identified my name with me. This identification is circular; it is closed; I have no identity beyond myself. When one identifies only with himself, he is lost to anything beyond himself. He loses his better selfhood in his limited image of himself.

Am I Somebody Special?

The point is this: We are all a bunch of nobodies—unless the reference point of our identity is outside ourselves. Some argue that every human has innate capacities that make him inherently important and worthwhile. But I respond: He has capacities *for what?* The capacity must be for something beyond himself. One example is that a person has the ability to think; he thinks about something outside himself. Thinking extends a person and takes him beyond himself. Even when he is thinking of himself, he has to step outside himself and make himself an object distinct from the subject who is doing the thinking.

Leon Spinks could say, "I am the boxing champ." This makes him somebody with reference to boxing. His identification point is outside himself. A politician can say, "I'm a senator, or a governor, or a United States President." This makes him something worthwhile beyond himself.

Someone says, "I'm a successful businessman," and another, "I'm a respected citizen in my community." Someone else says, "I'm Miss America," and still another, "I'm a celebrity in show biz." Each of these statements identifies the subject outside himself.

Most people are plagued with an almost insatiable thirst to be somebody special. We resort to a search for recognition, popularity or fame, and the drive becomes compulsive. We compromise our principles, lower our standards and cut corners on God. We even trample over others in our upward climb.

But most of us will never become celebrities. Unless we find a way to feel important apart from the acclaim of the world, we will forever be engaged in an exercise in futility. The craving for fame merely produces frustration.

Even those who do achieve the fanfare of the world often discover it does not satisfy; they find they have apparently been created for greater distinction than worldly applause. After he had achieved fame, one astronaut said, "I volunteered for Project Mercury because it was a chance for immortality. Most men never have that chance. But where does one go from immortality? Fame has the value and life expectancy of a bright patch on a wornout jacket."[2]

If what you do in the ring determines who you are outside the ring, you must outperform every fighter to remain anybody worth bragging about. If you identify only as a boxing champ, your being somebody depends on your remaining champ. As soon as you lose, you are a nobody. You may still say, "I *was* boxing king at one time." But that is like saying, "I used to be somebody worth talking about, but now I have lost my credentials for distinction."

If your only claim to fame is being senator, you lose that claim as soon as you lose the reelection race—or when the Committee on Ethics finds snakes in your

[2]Quoted by Billy Graham, "My Answer," Marion, Ind. *Chronicle-Tribune*, 8 February 1972, p. 5.

organization. If your highest identification is as a good business man, you lose most of your significance as soon as you have financial problems. If being a respected citizen in your community is your highest boast, you have to stay in your own community for boasting rights. It almost strikes me as cruel to refer to someone as "former" Miss America. Who wants to be a has-been? Sooner or later those perfect measurements will settle and the stunning cheekbones or chin will need a facelift.

Important to God

In order to be permanently and forever someone special and worthwhile, our identity must be with something—Someone—who is absolute and will never give way. And our identification with that Someone must remain constant and unending.

That swollen desire for applause reflects in part our loss of the high and holy position for which God has made us. When we lose our position as a child of God we lose our feelings of distinction, uniqueness and importance in the universe. If I am important to God, then I am important. I have value independent of my performance, good looks or bank account. But if I am nothing to God, all the acclaim of the world cannot satisfy my need to feel like somebody special. When I identify with Him, I am somebody. But if my greatest identity is with anything less than God, sooner or later that something will change, my identity will be undermined, and I will become a nobody. I will have lost my only source for adequate self-esteem.

In another *Peanuts* strip Lucy is parked in her psychiatric booth, and Charlie Brown is sharing his problems with her. "Sometimes I ask myself questions," he begins. "Sometimes I ask myself, 'Is this your real life, or is this just a pilot film?' Is my life a thirty-nine-week series or is it a special?" In no time at all Lucy analyzes his problem and gives an instant answer: "Whatever it is, your ratings are down. Five cents, please!"

Without Lucy's special permission, I want to answer every Charlie Brown in the world. Yes, this is your real life. No, it is not a pilot film. Yes, it is a special—it is very special!

Your life has been produced by the Great Producer for prime time. It is unique, different from any other program the world has ever viewed. You are very important to God. The production of your life was such a big project to God that when the script got all messed up He sent His own Son to rewrite it. When some would have scrapped the entire project, God sent Jesus to salvage His plan for your life. You are very special.

If you are craving the applause of the world, relax. God is in your fan club. You are important without having to try to be important—because you are important to Him.

Your ratings may be down by your viewing audience in the world. Your ratings may even have fallen in your own self-esteem, for having lost respect for yourself you do not enjoy yourself as you once did. But you are still popular with God. Though you have failed Him in so many ways, God is so interested in you that he is watching every move you make. The showing of your life is live and in color. Congratulations!

Move over, Hollywood. No thank you, Madison Avenue. I have God going for me. That is all I need.

If I am important to God, if I am the chosen of God, if I am loved by God, then I am important. I can stand ten feet tall. I can look anyone on earth straight in the eye. I can let my whole weight down on what I really am. I can relax being *me!* I have become the person I was created to be. I do not have to take a step backward for any person.

Though I lose every point of identity that made me something special in the world, I am still somebody in the universe—because I am somebody to God.

Leon Spinks, you are no longer boxing champ. But you need never be nobody again. God loves you, and you can belong to Him. Don't sell yourself short. You can forever be somebody bigger than world champion. Who are you? If you have accepted Him, you are God's child—that's who you are!

6
Moral Authority

Hold your breath for this teen-aged girl. Her psychological needs exploded all over Ann Landers' column in her protests against her parents. She had been cheated, not out of a nice home or a good car or adequate clothes or special privileges. She had been cheated by her parents—out of the privilege of being disciplined.

"I try to do the right thing," she wrote, "but it isn't easy when I know I don't have to answer to anybody. I have no respect for my parents because they have no power over me." She added, "Kids respect power."[1]

The Security of Authority

My wife, Sheila, and I have noticed how our children seem to gain emotional security when they are made to feel subject to parental authority. Many times our preschool-aged Marisa showed stress and tension in her eagerness to persuade us to let her visit a friend, or eat candy, or stay up late. As long as we were indecisive and

---

[1]Ann Landers' column, in [Lexington, Ky.] *Sunday Herald-Leader*, 5 November 1972.

allowed her to beg, her anxiety increased. One would expect her mental turmoil to subside as soon as we were persuaded to grant the permission. But the surprising thing is this: When we gave an authoritative "no" that left no room for further negotiating, she often gained a mental relaxation and emotional stability that was impossible until the matter was closed.

A child is not emotionally adequate to make all his/her own decisions. He is not equipped to handle such responsibility. Emotional security for him requires outside authority.

Somewhere below the surface of our adult confidence and sophistication, we all have within us a little child. The child I used to be is still within me, and the limitations I felt then are still felt from time to time. These feelings of inadequacy are consistent with reality, because I just happen to be limited in certain areas. It is only appropriate that I should *feel* ill-equipped to do that for which I *am* ill-equipped. This is especially true in matters of moral ethics.

In earlier chapters I have noted how we are created as social, physical and spiritual creatures. In this chapter we are looking at man as a moral creature and seeing how when his moral requirements are not fulfilled he becomes emotionally insecure.

It is so difficult to get it through our thick skulls that we are created creatures rather than creator, and that our existence is derived rather than self-produced. When we come to accept this as an axiom, however, it has far-reaching repercussions, spreading like shock waves through every area of our lives. The foundation of our philosophy is drastically shifted.

At the point of ethics it means two things. First, being creature rather than creator, having dependent existence rather than independent, we are *subject to* an authority higher than ourselves. We often come to recognize this with great reluctance, even with resistance, kicking our heels like spoiled children, breathing out profanities, determined to be subject to no authority higher than ourselves. But God is God, and that very fact requires subjection and obedience on our part. We cannot forever eliminate God from His universe to make room for our self-patronizing standards without Him. God steps into our moral vacuum and good becomes right and evil becomes wrong. We are accountable to the Source of our existence for the way we handle our trust.

The Moral Dilemma

Second, being created individuals, we *need* an authority beyond ourselves. At this point we find ourselves in a kind of dilemma. On one hand we are created *by* God, and on the other we are created *for* God. Being created by God, we are dependent on an outside source for our existence, which means we are finite rather than infinite. But being created for God means we have transcendent spirits. There is therefore a tension between the finiteness of our beings and the transcendence of our spirits.

The dilemma is this. Being finite we have within ourselves no adequate resource for absolute value. But being transcendent in spirit, we require moral values that are absolute, for a human-centered ethic is inadequate for a transcendent spirit. Feeling emotionally that we have been made for God, we are never emotionally at home in God's moral universe apart from a God-centered morality. For moral creatures, emotional fulfillment is impossible without moral fulfillment.

As long as we are responsible only to ourselves, we have no moral purpose outside ourselves, so we are not morally at home with ourselves. We are left emotionally disconnected and anchorless. But because our existence is not self-contained, we can have no permanent emotional security apart from outside authority.

In a way, we are made for God like an automobile is made for a driver. The car has to depend on a driver even to get started, and then it requires a driver to prevent it from wrecking itself. Like a runaway automobile, we may go for a short while without God in control. But we are on a collision course. Sooner or later we will crash. We need Someone bigger than ourselves operating the controls. We need God behind the steering wheel of our lives.

But God is not God over us at all unless HE is God in the realm of right and wrong. God by definition includes the notion of moral authority. As a physical creature I need God as Provider and Sustainer of life. As a social creature I need God as Father. As a spiritual creature I need God as Savior. But as a moral creature I need God as Authority.

The other day I heard a television personality boast, "With me anything goes. I am totally uninhibited. I can do as I please." When a person is subject only to himself, however, he is playing god. The screen star in substance was saying, "I am my own god."

But we are not morally big enough to be our own gods. Without God as our God, we become anxious and feel the insecurity of anchorlessness and homelessness. Made for a God so much bigger than ourselves, we are never morally adequate for ourselves. Going on a perpetual flashing yellow can give us ulcers. We need the security of a red light or a green light. Emotional security requires moral certainties.

We all have moral decisions to make. A high school student is choosing his lifestyle. A businessman is under pressure to comply with company practice. A teen-age girl discovers a civil war between her conscience and the pressures of her social group. A political official is tempted to make decisions based only on political expediency. The pressures of these moral decisions keep reminding us that we are moral creatures. We need moral guidelines that can structure our lives, acknowledging that we belong to a morally alive universe. Only in God can we find the moral authority to hold our lives together.

The Problem of Guilt

Since man is a moral creature with moral sensitivity and some kind of moral standard, he has become victimized by guilt. Anthropologists have found among all cultures two things—a sense of moral oughtness and a feeling of guilt from violating that oughtness.

A suffocating sense of guilt has smothered its victims like spiritual smog. Driven by relentless emotional pressure, such people have gone to great trouble to escape this mental cloud. Some have belittled themselves, punished themselves, made religious sacrifices, hoping they can outsacrifice the weightiness of their moral offenses.

In so doing, they have run up against two unsolvable emotional problems. First, their sins are always emotionally before them, always outweighing their sacrifice.

Yes, I know today there is the tendency to bolster one's self-image by boasting about sin. There is a certain prestige attached to being "a man of the world," so profanity and promiscuity have become symbols of status. We hear persons brag about their sins, and we see them shy away from being thought of as good or saintly.

Yet in the presence of goodness and rightness those who are morally guilty recoil. The sin that looked cute and courageous begins to look ugly and distasteful when goodness walks on the scene. A prostitute tries to make herself look appealing, but standing beside a virgin her prostitution looks utterly disdainful. In the presence of goodness the feeling persists that moral discrepancies are not cute little naughty things that give zing, zest and gusto to life, but that they are grievous sins—cosmic crimes.

The second emotional problem is this. If man by sacrificing should be able to compensate for his sins, the atonement would fall short of the emotional support inherent in the concept of divine forgiveness.

The person who feels guilt needs two things. He needs emotional freedom from the guilt, and because he feels his sins are against God, he needs the emotional support of divine forgiveness. He needs his sins atoned for, but he needs to feel more than just a balanced record sheet. When I have spanked my children, they feel the penalty has been imposed for their offense and that they are absolved. But this never seems to satisfy them emotionally. They always want to hug, to be cuddled and to "make up." They want a reconciliation of the fellowship.

Other major religions attempt to offer freedom from the guilt of sin, though many of their adherents would deny feeling the release from guilt. But the Christian faith offers a restoration of fellowship with God, the feeling of divine favor, the emotional support of divine forgiveness.

Divine Forgiveness

The emotional problem that is often experienced in seeking a freely-given forgiveness, however, is the first problem of feeling freedom from the guilt. A lot has been made of the emotional need to earn one's own clean record. Forgiveness seems cheap—too light to counterbalance the weightiness of one's sins. So the person feels forgiveness, but he still feels guilty. And the offense of his sins seems so heavy that he can never quite earn the release he wants.

What he needs psychologically is a costly forgiveness, an expensive pardon, a *sacrificial* divine willingness to absolve the guilt. He needs a forgiveness with weightiness equal to the gravity of his sins. Then he can set out to bolster his moral self-image by keeping his record clean. But he can feel the emotional support of a *costly* divine forgiveness.

This kind of forgiveness we find in the death of Jesus. At the cross our sinfulness was confronting God's holiness, and the awful confrontation was resolved. At Calvary we do not see God taking our sins lightly. The forgiveness He offers is not cheap and superficial. It was a costly thing for Him. It is a prize we should treasure above any earthly possession. It is too expensive for us to purchase and too weighty for God to grant freely without sacrifice on His part.

At the cross of Christ I find divine forgiveness freely granted, providing for me the emotional support that I need. And at the same cross I discover a sacrifice that outweighs the heaviness of my sins, making the forgiveness authentic, and giving me an emotional relief from guilt.

7
Made to Be Mastered

How on earth do you give a talk on Christian freedom to inmates in a jail?

My first such attempt was during my student days, and I had very little appreciation for freedom—because I had never known the bondage these men knew. The meeting began with a group of college students making a rather sad effort at singing. Then a seminary student offered a holier-than-thou prayer, and another read a long genealogy of unpronounceable names from First Chronicles and invoked the blessing of God on his reading of Holy Scripture. Now it was my time to give my talk on the bondage of sin and the freedom one can find in Christ.

The jail had the dirtiest, dingiest cells I have ever beheld. The men were respectful during my talk, but as soon as I finished a shabby, unshaven inmate blurted out, "Can God get me out of jail?" He was quiet during my theological explanation, but then he put it to me straight: "Will *you* get me out?"

Since that experience it has been my privilege to talk with many inmates in several state prisons and many local jails, but my heart always hurts with the confinement these men feel. After I spoke to a group of prisoners in the federal prison of Cuba on the Isle of Pines, some of them wanted to know what it was like to be a free American. I gave a talk to the patients confined to a leprosy colony in the Bahamas, and as I left their longing eyes followed me outside the camp. I was free. But they remained.

Personality Prisons

After sharing with so many prisoners, I began to make a discovery. Surprisingly, I found that most of the inmates were confined by barriers more formidable than the steel bars of their cells. They were behind bars built into their own personalities, living in emotional lockups that were darker and dingier than the prison cells they occupied.

A second discovery was even more revealing. Those who have never been in the correctional institutions of society are locked in the very same kind of personality prisons.

Mrs. Jones is hooked on a habit that she cannot kick. Mr. Brown is hung up on a personality pattern that will not let him go. The younger Wilson son is locked up in a lifestyle to which he has become a slave, and he cannot shake loose. The Mitchell daughter has developed patterns of feeling and reacting that bind her like chains, and she cannot break out. They have all tried so valiantly so often only to stumble and fall again. Even their firmest resolves have been broken. Now all the promises they make to themselves seem empty. Repeated failure has shattered their faith in themselves. Their emotions are bruised with guilt, fear, unpleasant memories and feelings of inadequacy, and these damaged emotions in turn become habitual and binding. Such people keep hoping for freedom, but their lives keep imprisoning them, like some broken record playing the same sad phrase over and again.

Emotional scars can be found inside all of us. For some it is a deep hurt, a deep hate or a deep fear. For others it is a supersensitivity which binds them as slaves, directs their attitudes and controls their lives. Patterns develop within their personalities as they attempt to cope with misdirected impulses in meeting basic emotional needs. And these patterns become enslaving.

Now here was a third discovery. The bondage I discovered in others was precisely the same bondage I had overlooked in myself. I was supposed to be free, observing others objectively. Yet in many ways I was enslaved by personality patterns that drove me as ruthlessly as a slave driver.

No Freedom Without Bondage

It all added up to an obvious principle that runs throughout the human race—every person is in many ways a slave. There simply is no way to exist as a human being apart from a measure of bondage. The concept of freedom without boundaries is a false concept. A train is free to run only as it is "enslaved" by the tracks. The human personality is structured so as to require a master. Without this structure the personality disintegrates.

Though he often does not recognize it, man's attitudes and behavior indicate a desire to be subject to something outside himself—home, family, community, clubs, large business corporations, social institutions. Over 900 people were so unnerved by an unstructured world that they followed Jim Jones to his colony in Guyana. In their need to be mastered, they surrendered their freedom, and were freed from the pressures of living without restraint. Their need for subjection to a structured society ended in mass suicide.

Some inmates actually feel more secure in prison than in the open freedom of society. In the bondage of prison they are given a measure of freedom from themselves, from compulsive emotional drives and enslaving personality patterns. In other words, they find freedom *not* to commit crime. All people need restricting boundaries, and if they are not equipped with self-discipline, they need arbitrary structures. Either way, human emotions need to be mastered.

Similarly, man feels he should belong to beauty, to love, to truth. His emotional nature demands the feeling of belonging to something transcendent. Instinctively and intuitively he feels inadequate for himself. This reflects man's created nature, derived and dependent and therefore insufficient in itself. We are made to be mastered.

The maxim is this: We will be mastered by *something;* emotional survival requires it. We are made that way. But because we have the awesome potential to be mastered by goodness and God, we carry with us a frightening vulnerability to the bondage of evil. While we are built with a tendency toward God, we have acquired an alien propensity to react against the lordship of God. In attempting to extricate ourselves from bondage to the good, we have become enslaved to the bad. Every disentanglement from one bondage places us in another bondage.

We want to be free, so we are free to become gluttons— we become slaves to obesity. Tim threw off all parental restraints and felt free to smoke, but he became a slave to nicotine and then to lung cancer. Tim's father felt free to drink, but he became a slave to alcoholism, then to a frayed nervous system, then to a broken home, then a diseased body, then death. Tim's sister felt free to pursue what she called "free love," but she had a baby she could not support and had to take a job she did not want. When she got a little older, her "free lovers" passed her by for younger women. She was left without real love, and became a slave to guilt, loneliness and a broken heart. In the name of freedom we are becoming slaves!

You cannot avoid the fact that causes have effects that are binding. Acts entail consequences that are enslaving. Present choices determine destinies that are irreversible. Freedom to act is not freedom from the consequence of the action. When you exercise your privilege to live as you please, you lose your privilege to die as you please. God gave man a measure of freedom, and man has used that freedom to enslave himself and eventually to destroy himself.

Self, a Ruthless Master

A person gets so tangled up with what he likes that he is not free to do what he does not like. A large landowner wants to be free to acquire large tracts of real estate. He wants to be owner of expensive property. But he becomes so emotionally involved in what belongs to him that he ends up belonging to what he has. The land owns him more than he owns the land. This is not freedom; this is bondage! If in the name of liberty we are seeking license to do as we please, we will become more and more enslaved.

A high school girl begged her mother, "Help me! I

don't want to do what I want to do!" This was not a contradiction; she was eloquently expressing the bondage that enslaves millions of people.

There is no greater imprisonment than being behind one's own prison bars. Tim cannot be free from his enslaving habit simply because he does not *want* to be free as much as he wants to be enslaved. We are bound by the wants and desires that we develop in being free. We get tied up in knots with ourselves. The biggest hangup I will ever have is with the person who walks in my shoes, wears my face and bears my name. By being myself, I am in a position to be my own greatest enemy and to cause my own greatest defeat.

According to some typewriter repairmen, the one key that often wears out first is the letter I. They surmise the reason is not that the key is hit more often than the others, but that it is consistently hit harder than the rest of them.

If we could only be freed from those egocentric drives of self-will and self-glorification, how free we would be! This is what hell is all about—a person so wrapped up in himself that he is permanently enslaved to himself.

My friends in Zimbabwe have told me how the local people trap monkeys in that part of Africa. A hole is bored in a gourd just large enough for a monkey's hand, and kernels of corn are placed inside. Then the gourd is tied to the foot of a tree. When the monkeys come down the tree, one of them will slip a hand inside the gourd and scoop up the corn. But with its fist clenched around the grain, it cannot slip its hand out. All it would have to do to be free is to let go of the grain, but it flatly refuses to let go. It is trapped by its own greed, enslaved by its own selfishness . . .

. . . in much the same way that we humans become enslaved to ourselves. No person is ever truly free until he is free to live without that which he selfishly wants most. In the last chapter I spoke of the emotional security that comes in being subject to moral authority. Here I am speaking of the emotional freedom that comes in being in the right kind of bondage.

The Emancipation Proclamation

Because we are made to be mastered, there can be no freedom without bondage. The question then is not whether there is freedom, but what kind of bondage. It is not *who* you are, but *whose* you are.

In one way or another we have all been captured by ourselves. We have come into the worst kind of bondage —slavery to self. And we cannot dethrone ourselves from being lord over ourselves.

We can only be free from ourselves when we are mastered by Someone big enough to be our master— Someone big enough to free us from all lesser bondage. Only God is big enough to be Lord and Master over us. As big and important as we are and as enslaved as we have become to ourselves, we require nothing less than God as a master. No person is free by getting God "off his back." Freedom from God makes us vulnerable to the worst sort of bondage. But a voluntary bondage to God liberates from the slavery imposed by every smaller master in life.

There is an emancipation proclamation written into the Christian gospel. In Christ we find freedom to tran-scend ourselves and our selfish desires, freedom to rise above our worse selves and freedom to become our better selves. We become slaves—love-slaves—to Christ, and we are freed from slavery to ourselves. We are made to be free—by being mastered.

Here is my big discovery. Freedom comes in the *willingness* to be a slave. When the center of gravity in

our lives is shifted from self to Christ, we have the
foundation for freedom from every emotion that has
enslaved us.

Perhaps this is what Jesus meant when he said, "For
whosoever will save his life shall lose it: and whosoever
will lose his life for my sake shall find it" (Matt. 16:25).
Certainly this is what George Matheson meant in his
great hymn:

> Make me a captive, Lord,
>   And then I shall be free;
> Force me to render up my sword,
>   And I shall conqueror be . . .
>
> My will is not my own
>   Till Thou hast made it Thine;
> If it would reach a monarch's throne
>   It must its crown resign . . .

8
A Transcendent Purpose

Walking on the moon was too much for one of our astronauts. For years moon walking had been his greatest goal in life, and he labored tirelessly toward achieving that goal. But once it was attained, he explained, there was no higher goal and he became disillusioned. He lost his ambition and his drive. Finally he suffered an emotional breakdown.

For another astronaut, however, the moon visit meant something totally different. In his autobiography, *To Rule the Night*, James Irwin wrote, "As we flew into space we had a new sense of ourselves, of the earth and of the nearness to God. We were outside ordinary reality; I sensed the beginning of some sort of deep change taking place inside of me."

Irwin continued, "The ultimate effect has been to deepen and strengthen all the religious insight I ever had. . . . On the moon the total picture of the power of God and his Son Jesus Christ became abundantly clear to me."[1]

[1]James B. Irwin and William A. Emerson, Jr., *To Rule the Night: The Discovery Voyage of Astronaut Jim Irwin* (Philadelphia: A. J. Holman Co., 1973).

James Irwin was able to cut through a million technical details of his mission and experience God. He saw beyond the moon to the God who made the moon, and the lunar surface on which he stood was holy ground.

One astronaut experienced confusion, emotional disturbance and unrest. The other discovered the reality of God in a new way. One saw his own accomplishment in getting to the moon. The other saw beyond himself to the God who helped him reach the moon. One saw the moon as his highest goal, but the goal was too low. He cracked and broke. The other had a bigger goal than the moon to live for and a higher goal than reaching the moon to strive for. He had a purpose beyond his own achievements.

Both men had been created for a goal higher than moon walking. One traded his higher goal for an absolute commitment to the lower goal, and it was not adequate to sustain him. The other was anchored in a higher goal, and that turned the lunar-stroll goal into an exciting and meaningful experience.

Man's Greatest Need . . .

In chapter one I touched on the human need for an adequate purpose. As great as our social problems in America are today, the greatest problem is not poverty, unemployment, or pollution; it is not physical, social or economic. Our greatest plague is an emotional deficit resulting from a poverty of spirit. The greatest problem is meaninglessness; we are surrounded by material wealth and have nothing to live for. Millions of lives are revolving around a hub of emptiness and purposelessness. Indeed, affluence serves only to divert temporarily our attention from our crisis in meaning.

The ultimate purpose in life for so many people is

simply to stay alive. Someone says, "After all, my first obligation is to make a living." Certainly survival is not a goal to be disparaged; it is more worthy than living merely for pleasure, luxuries or power over others. But as one's highest goal, survival is inadequate for the emotional needs of the human spirit—on three counts.

First, the goal is unreachable because permanent survival in this world is impossible. And a goal that is unreachable is frustrating. You spend your entire life on one thing—survival—and then you do not survive. Your purpose in life betrays you and mocks you. It lets you down, because you are striving against the inevitable—death.

Second, the goal of mere survival is no higher than that found in the animal kingdom. When staying alive becomes your highest goal, your purpose in life is lowered to that of a squirrel or a mouse. Then your spirit shrivels up, your soul becomes anemic, your personality is impoverished. The purpose is not big enough for a creature with your kind of spirit. It does not give sufficient emotional satisfaction.

Third, when survival is your highest goal, you are living for nothing more than living. This is like the small farmer who kept his mules to raise a crop, and raised a crop to be able to feed his mules. You live so you can be alive, and you stay alive so you can live. This is like a cat chasing its own tail. You are living in a meaningless circle. Life becomes redundant, turned in on itself.

Life cannot exist for long unless it exists for something beyond itself. Life is trivial when it has no purpose beyond itself, and the human personality cannot survive on triviality. Because our souls were made for a higher purpose than mere survival, we cannot permanently survive with survival as a goal.

. . . A God-centered Goal

Since man has not been created by himself, the purpose of his existence is not found within himself. The purpose of my life can only be found in the One who gave me life.

Somehow my spirit refuses to believe my life is a big mistake. My emotions cannot live with that. Emotional health requires a purpose to my existence. If God created me, He had a purpose in this unusual project. I am made for His purpose, and I can never be fulfilled until I find my purpose in Him. Every lesser goal in life leaves me living below my potential, settling for less than I have been made for. Having been made for the ultimate, my spirit can never be quite satisfied with the immediate. Made for the eternal, I become bored with no goal beyond the temporal.

When I can see no meaning beyond my present life, I feel like a big bundle of contradictions. I have no master purpose to unify my lesser goals and values. Made for something bigger than *me*, I am never adequate for *me*. My soul keeps saying, "I was made for God. Don't shortchange me. Give me God!" Without God to live for, my soul is forever tormented with *me*. I am just not a big enough goal for a person as big as I. For my own satisfaction, I require a God-centered goal.

There is only one purpose high enough to be worthy of you. That purpose is well within reach. It is to live for God and to be preoccupied with pleasing Him. There is a paradox in this, however. Human emotions need this purpose in order to satisfy the human spirit. But the purpose must be chosen primarily for God's sake, with no more than a secondary consideration for emotional requirements. Otherwise the ulterior motive eclipses the higher motive that is necessary to please God. Wanting to please God more than you want to please yourself, ironically, is the only way to be able to please yourself. When you *want* to do what He wants you to do more than what you want to do, you can, paradoxically, do anything you want to do. This is a lifestyle beyond yourself, and it is both liberating and exciting.

This higher purpose transcends all other purposes, and it alone is enough to provide emotional satisfaction and fulfillment when our lower goals are unreached. Jesus lost human comforts, friends and His own reputation, but He remained secure and at peace. He had said, "I seek not mine own will, but the will of the Father" (John 5:30). No lesser goal than pleasing God, no smaller purpose than the purpose of God, can capture our hearts and absorb our interests in a permanently satisfying way.

One astronaut reached the moon and saw how important he was, now that he had reached the moon. But James Irwin reached the moon and saw how little he was in God's great cosmos. One could not see God because he saw himself as being so big. The other saw beyond himself to the God behind it all. One was so wrapped up in his self-centered goal that he missed God. The other stood taller than himself and rose above himself—and he experienced God.

It is a beautiful thing. Our emotional needs square so perfectly with God's purposes for us. Surely they were made for each other.

9
Suffering Must Have Meaning

When Jim and Marilynn Foulkes committed their lives to be medical missionaries in Africa, they had no idea what that would entail.

Certainly, they expected hardships and opposition. They knew this kind of lifestyle would be relentless in its demands for sacrifice. It would include personal discipline in medical and language preparation, a high level of emotional maturity to withstand cultural shock and to cope with the frustrations only a missionary knows. Above all, devotion, dedication and commitment were imperative.

What they did not know was that they would bury a son in Zambia. They did not know their sixteen-year-old daughter would suffer extended pain and trauma from an undiagnosed disease before her ravaged body would finally be placed in Zambian soil near her brother. Nor did Dr. Jim Foulkes know his wife's health would be destroyed by an aggressive illness when she was only in her mid-forties—and that her body, too, would be left below African sod.

Jim Foulkes' earlier sacrifice had been beyond expression. And then, this! If it had happened to you and me, most of us would have reacted, "Why me, God?" We would wonder whether evil is always returned for good and sacrifice rewarded with heartbreak. Was John Greenleaf Whittier wrong when he wrote, "Life is ever lord of death, And love can never lose its own"?

Why Suffering?

From our human standpoint the tragedies of life are absurd, nonsensical and meaningless. Why should twelve missionary family members be brutally hacked to death by terrorist guerrillas in Zimbabwe? Is the package of life only a bundle of contradictions? In view of the seemingly ludicrous and incongruent events of life, this world looks like an insane asylum being run by the inmates.

For centuries, in the aftermath of tragedies people have asked, "Why?" The question is not irrelevant. It is an appropriate question to be asked by rational minds. It is a philosophical question, of course, but the answer has an unmistakable psychological bearing on the human personality.

A person is an entity with both mind and emotions. The two are categorically distinct, but they interact within the personality. We have rational minds— notwithstanding our frequent irrationality—and our emotions are not comfortable with irrational answers.

Not only do we want rational answers, but we desire ultimate answers. Our emotions need answers that have some reference to the absolute. We have difficulty being satisfied with answers that are given in the relative framework of our temporary existence on earth.

Perhaps this is the reason questions about suffering have often been asked and answered with reference to God. Even skeptics have used the problem of suffering to reflect on either God's existence or His goodness. To speak of human suffering in terms of God is to assume that pain is either intrinsically evil or intrinsically good, and this is yet to be proved. The question "Why?" suggests there is a reason, however, and it is usually intended to suggest God had a reason for it to happen.

When British missionaries were savagely slaughtered in Zimbabwe, the Associated Press quoted some religionists as saying God had a reason to take the missionaries. This attitude might have given some emotional support for those nearest the tragedy, but it violates both a scriptural and a rational image of God. It placates emotions by appealing to an ultimate answer, but it in no way gives a rational answer.

I am appalled at the way God is so often blamed for the wicked, terrifying atrocities of evil men! Can anyone really believe that God put those killers up to that barbaric crime? Why should the blame for the brutal acts of madmen be pinned on God?

Someone argues, "But God is supposed to be in charge of everything." Then my response is, "How so, and who said?" This would make robots out of people and leave them with no freedom at all. This is not the way God has set up his governing system in the world. He has temporarily given people freedom of authority over their own actions. In order to grant this freedom God is logically required to permit many things that He does not purpose. To say God purposed the terrorist killings is to say the killers themselves are not responsible.

But tragedies are not only human-caused; there are also accidents and diseases that appear to be totally senseless, without rhyme or reason. And this is precisely why they are called accidents—because no purpose behind them can be found. An accident is a happening for which no purpose can be assigned.

Emotional Satisfaction

In order to find adequate emotional support for tragedy, we need to make two valid distinctions.

First, there is a difference between the *cause* of an event and the *purpose* of an event. The cause suggests a prior set of circumstances out of which the event takes place. The purpose has to do with the goal toward which the event moves. Now every accident has a cause, but it does not have a purpose. The diseases that took the lives of Jim Foulkes' family were definitely caused, but this is a far cry from saying God had a reason for the deaths to happen.

Second, we need to distinguish between what is God's purpose *for* something and what is God's purpose *in* something. There is a difference between what God purposes to happen and how God can use for His own purposes what has happened. He can bring good out of bad when He did not wish the bad to happen at all. To say God *can find* a purpose *in* a situation is not to say he *had* a purpose *for* the situation. He can even find a way for a death to serve His purpose when He did not purpose the death to happen at all. The psalmist exclaimed, "Surely the wrath of men shall praise thee" (Ps. 76:10, RSV).

In an earlier chapter I spoke of the need for a purpose in life that is big enough to hold life together in spite of tragedy. Here I am saying the tragedy itself can work toward God's good purposes in your life. Ten thousand things may happen to you that were not God's original intention, but out of every bad thing will emerge a good thing—and God's purposes will be served.

From her dad's illness my daughter developed a sympathetic attitude toward those who are ill. God did not purpose my illness, but He did purpose the attitude of sympathy in my daughter. So God used what was not His purpose to serve His purpose. My illness therefore was not wasted. He used a hospital experience to teach me patience. He used an automobile accident to teach me caution. He used a disappointment to teach me sympathy. My tears were used to make me tender. My hurt was used to make me more humane.

Life is hurling daggers at all of us in various ways. We can seize them by the blade with self-pity, and we will be injured. But every dagger has a handle on it. If we have the courage and faith to find the handle, we can take the worst that life can do and make out of it the very best.

Earlier I spoke about being free from self by belonging to God, and I discussed having one's highest purpose in God. These are prerequisites for dealing emotionally with suffering. If we belong to Him, life's agonizing crises are not ours, but His. Instead of ours to lament, they are His to employ.

We get emotional support and satisfaction at this point in suffering. When life's problems are being used, they are not being wasted. This takes from our emotions the feeling of futility. Though suffering is not intended, it is useful. Though it is not purposed, it is purposeful. The questions may not all be answered, but the contradiction is resolved. If God can be glorified through the suffering, then the suffering is being used. When it is being used, it is not lost. It is no longer senseless. It gains significance and meaning. There is sense in suffering.

Thus Jim Foulkes, after burying a son, a daughter and a wife in Africa, could say, "It is impossible for me to express the praise I have in my heart to God."[1] He was surrendered to God's ultimate purpose in his life, and the beauty of that commitment shone bright through tears of grief.

It was that commitment to God's purpose that gave significance to Jim Foulkes' suffering. He not only had purpose in life in spite of the loss—he knew that the tragedy itself would be used for higher purposes. The futility he felt was overcome by a feeling of meaningfulness and worthwhileness. The loss was not in vain.

[1]Quoted in *Asbury College Ambassador* (Wilmore, Ky; Spring 1978), pp. 4–6.

10
Handling Failure

My heart hurt for my friend Mike. He had lost his wife in divorce and had lost the respect of his children. He had flunked a qualifying exam for a position he had set his heart on. Large investments and several years were lost when his business bottomed out.

But these were not his problem. Failures in life can most often be handled from a practical standpoint more easily than they can be handled emotionally. Mike was punishing himself with self-accusation. In his repeated failure he had lost confidence and self-respect. Each defeat intensified the obsession for victory, and the obsession made the next failure more devastating. Now he was demoralized and paralyzed with disappointment.

Mike had a toothpaste-ad smile that concealed his bleeding heart. Nobody knew it, but in secret he had wept until his eyes had no more tears. His disappointment had marked his personality like chiseled grooves in granite. Outwardly he held his chin up, but inwardly he slumped.

Victory Beyond Defeat

To be human is to be victim of failure in one way or another. The circumstances of failure cannot always be changed, because contributing causes are often beyond our control. For this reason, we need to be God-equipped to handle the failure we either could not or did not prevent. This is the only way to handle it in a way that will give a kind of victory over ourselves and over our feelings in spite of the defeat.

The equipment that God gives, however, is not so much emotional as it is moral and mental. What we need is not the emotion that can handle failure as much as we need the character that can handle emotion in time of failure. Emotions do not cope with failure. It is *people* who cope *emotionally* with their failure by refusing to allow their emotions to control them.

The nature of emotion is to respond negatively to defeat. Negative response is emotionally appropriate for negative situations. When my neighbor does not appear to react negatively to failure, I first believe he is emotionally healthy. But upon closer scrutiny I discover his emotions are not necessarily either healthy or unhealthy. It is his character that is healthy enough to discipline his emotions. Left alone, emotions by nature respond appropriately—negative to negative and positive to positive.

A few days after Muhammad Ali first lost to Joe Fraser the world heavyweight boxing title, I was watching Ali being interviewed on a television talk show. He said something that grabbed me in the chest, though for some reason the sports writers did not pick it up.

"In a way it was good that I was defeated," Ali said. "Real victory comes in being able to accept defeat." What an incredible way for a demolished champion to speak of his own defeat! Certainly Ali had feelings of regret and disappointment, for behind the mechanical precision that we see in the ring is a human soul with human feelings.

When I heard the talk show, I was not hearing the easy and automatic response of emotion. I was hearing a person who so disciplined his emotions on the occasion that he stood taller than the circumstance of his defeat. The emotions were under the control of a person who was under control. He had victory beyond his defeat.

This is where God comes in. Rather than equipping our emotions to handle defeat, he equips *us* to handle the defeat. Then we are in a position to cope emotionally with the failure, and we are given a victory beyond the defeat. There are at least three ways this works.

A Value Shift

First, by sharing life with God from day to day, my values shift quite automatically from a lesser value level to a greater. Most of our battles that absorb most of our interests are in areas that are without much value on the long haul. The glory of such victory is dimmed and the sting of defeat is blunted because the value of victory is so limited.

Muhammad Ali was saying there is a higher victory-value than winning in the boxing ring. Being able to control one's attitude and keep one's character intact is of greater value than controlling a boxing opponent. Gaining victory over oneself in defeat is greater than gaining victory over an enemy. Enjoying the smile of God is greater than basking in the applause of the world.

Furthermore, quite often it is defeat on the lower level that makes possible a greater victory on the higher level. Ali said he was the hero of millions who were constantly defeated in life, and it did them good to know their hero could be defeated too. Only by losing in the ring could he identify with them—thereby gaining a more worthwhile victory.

The greatest victory our world has ever known was the resurrection of Christ from the dead. But it was occasioned by the most horrible of all defeats—the crucifixion of the world's perfect Person. Could Christ ever have arisen from the dead if He had not first died? In that dark defeat of all defeats, the Son of God was winning a victory for each of us. By His death (what a defeat!) we have life (what a victory!).

When your values are shifted to the higher level, you can gain a victory not only in spite of your lower losses, but precisely because of them. God has now equipped your character with a value system that can handle your emotions in time of failure. The transcendent purpose gives you something to live for beyond the defeat. When your emotions are responding negatively to defeat on the lower level, you can switch your attention to your higher interests, where the emotions find something positive to respond to.

Attempting to reweave threadbare emotions without strengthening character and shifting values simply will not work. Therapy must begin with basics, and emotions must have an adequate foundation.

With a character' that is God-equipped with higher values, you can walk out of the boxing ring, beaten, defeated, demolished as a champ, and in your soul you can be champion over your own defeat.

A Higher Input

Second, living in voluntary conjunction with God furnishes an input to our lives higher than the situation in which we may have won victory or suffered defeat. The smile of God overcomes self-accusation; divine forgiveness dissolves guilt; God's love keeps us feeling important; His comfort gives emotional contentment.

His emotional support gives us victory over ourselves in a situation in which we are defeated.

Then your defeats do not defeat you, and you can live the victorious life. Living victoriously means relating everything that occurs—even your defeats—to the adequacy of Christ. Your defeats will be defeated!

Third, when we belong to God—at the center of personality where pretense is impossible—then our defeats are His, not ours. They lose their debilitating force. Adequate room is left for emotional survival—even emotional health.

When we committed ourselves to Him with rock-bottom honesty, in a way we got ourselves off our own hands. We had all to gain and nothing to lose in dumping our battered lives in His hands. He had all to lose and nothing to gain by accepting us. Now that we are His rather than our own, He gets the kickback from our failure. The meaning of the failure is changed from defeat to challenge. Our emotions can live with this kind of defeat.

You may lose a thousand battles, but if you are surrendered to God you will not lose the war. You can walk out into a world that has torn you to pieces—and stay healthy and whole. Bruised, beaten and battered, you need not be broken. In life's greatest defeat you will have victory.

My friend Mike now belongs to God. Out of repeated failure a victory has emerged that is quite new and invigorating. The failures have not been changed, but he has been changed. His values are different. He gets input from a higher Source. His emotions are intact, no longer victimized by his failures. There is inner relaxation and a sense of settledness. Instead of groveling in the past, Mike is living in the present and looking toward the future.

11
Handling Success

Week after week the veteran pedestrian trudged back to the drivers' testing office. One-hundred-three consecutive times she took the test. One-hundred-three consecutive times she failed.

The Associated Press carried the story of the seventy-five-year-old woman in Little Rock. In relentless pursuit of a driver's license she doggedly rejected defeat. She continued studying the manual. On the one-hundred-fourth attempt she passed the test. Today "Miss Fannie" is driving her car.

The best way to be on top of our defeat-vulnerable emotions is to gain a victory. Rather than attempting simply to find a way to accept our failures, we should make appropriate effort wherever possible to overcome the failure with success.

One of the greatest inventors of all time was taken out of school after three months' formal education, having been called "retarded" by his first grade teacher. But Thomas Edison invented the electric light, phonograph, movie camera and hundreds of other marvels.

So you and I passed our drivers' exam the first time, and our first grade teacher thought we were pretty bright.

Congratulations to us! But our tenacity does not inspire newspaper stories. And our inventions have not blessed the world.

The Lawrence Welk show is one of the longest-running programs on national television, and it has been consistently popular. Everybody knows that. But most people do not know that back in the 1930s in North Dakota Welk's entire band walked out on him because they thought he was not a good enough musician to make the big time. They all left. And what did Lawrence Welk do? He began assembling other musicians and organized another band. And look what happened: Few conductors have made it in a bigger way than he.

Most of us have striven so valiantly for so long, only to fall flat on our faces over and again. In the last chapter I talked about handling those failures emotionally that cannot be handled by success. In so doing one can become an emotional success even in failure.

Good Losers, Poor Winners

When the failure is overcome, however, all the related emotional problems may not be resolved. The success may just be harder for the emotions to cope with than the failure. Many people are no more equipped to handle victory than they are defeat. Indeed, it is sometimes easier to have courage for the storm than to have stability and grace for the calm after the storm. More people stumble in their leisure time than in their working hours, and probably more people have been drugged by success than conquered by failure.

It is often more difficult to be a good winner than a good loser. Many have been able to lose without pouting who have not had the emotional resources to win without bragging. In being poor winners, we "win" for ourselves a greater defeat—a failure that would not be possible apart from the victory. Simply by winning it is possible to set ourselves up emotionally to be defeated in a more serious way. We need the equipment to discipline our inflated moods as well as our depressed moods.

Many sports enthusiasts argue that Joe Louis in his prime was the most formidable boxing champion in history. Certainly he was among the greatest.

The irony of his life, however, is spelled out by Louis himself in his recent autobiography, *Joe Louis: My Life*.[1] "The women," he says, "came jumping at me. I was the weaker sex. I didn't resist one pretty girl who had a sparkle in her eye."

One after another, Joe Louis tells of his extra-marital affairs, hanging it all out for the world to read. He says these affairs led to drugs, and almost led him to murder one of his former lovers. "What made me do something like that?" he asks. The man who could deliver the knockout blow in the ring was himself kayoed in the moral ring of life.

When we are not emotionally equipped to handle victory, we condition ourselves for a greater kind of failure. Over-confidence, exaggerated pride, egocentric ambitions possess us and control us. We are driven to a dangerously inflated lifestyle. We become moral failures simply because we do not discipline ourselves to handle our victories adequately.

God-Provided Equipment

What is needed to handle success is the very same equipment that is needed for failure. It is moral and

---

[1]Joe Louis and Art Rust, *Joe Louis: My Life* (New York: Berkley Publishing Corp., 1981).

mental. We do not have as much problem with success as we have with the emotion associated with success. What we need is the character to handle the emotion we feel in situations of success. We need the character credentials to handle success without allowing the emotion of success to handle us.

The three pieces of God-provided equipment suggested in the last chapter for failure function in the same way for success.

First, the value shift that occurs naturally as we share life with God reduces the premium we place on success. It is not that success becomes unimportant, but it loses its priority status.

The football coach to whom "winning is everything" has nothing to fall back on emotionally when his team is defeated. But neither does he have anything of much value to bank on when his team has won a clobbering victory. Staking his highest goal in life to an athletic victory leaves him vulnerable to the instability of that success and ill equips his emotions for the value of higher level victory.

With a transcendent purpose, success can be enjoyed with grace and humility. Emotions are not inflated enough to be punctured. Our lives move on an even keel with dignity and balance.

Emotional Support

Second, the higher input we get from God furnishes an undergirding support that is solid and permanent. The emotional input of success fluctuates and falters, and makes for insecure and hesitating personalities. The emotional support of God is neither blown up with success nor deflated with failure. It is constant and lasting, and makes for emotional gravity, stability and security.

Third, when we belong to God on the deep level of our motives, we really have no claim to our successes. They are His, not ours. Consequently we have no reason to become abnormally proud or egocentric. The excessive feeling that creates personality instability is preempted. Our emotions are less subject to fluctuation.

Committed to Him, we become more God-centered than self-centered, so our successes are less self-serving and more glorifying to God. The emotion attached to success is liberating rather than binding because it is focused outside ourselves.

Earlier I spoke of being mastered by God. It is in this kind of belonging that we find the emotional equilibrium to have success without letting the success get us down.

12
Mastering Your Moods

Charles M. Schulz so realistically depicts human nature that I can hardly resist the temptation to refer to *Peanuts* again.

Lucy, the number-one crab of the comics, recently remarked, "Boy, do I feel crabby." Linus responded, "Maybe I can be of help. Why don't you just take my place here in front of the TV while I go and fix you a nice snack? Sometimes we all need a little pampering to help us feel better." When Linus returned with a sandwich, chocolate chip cookies and a glass of milk, he said, "Now, is there anything else I can get you? Is there anything I haven't thought of?"

Lucy took the tray of food and replied, "Yes, there's one thing you haven't thought of." Then she screamed, "I don't wanna feel better!"

Happiness or Crabbiness

The human personality is strange and paradoxical, often contradictory. Human emotions are vulnerable to all kinds of moods that we cannot quite unravel and understand. Our crabbiness makes us miserable, but we cherish the misery of crabbiness at the price of happiness.

In Young and Raymond's comic strip *Blondie*, Dagwood recently came home from the office saying, "I've never been in a worse mood!" Blondie met him at the door, kissed him and told him how much she loved him and had missed him. When Dagwood hung up his coat and hat, he said to himself, "She just ruined the best worse mood I ever had!"

Here is the chronic emotional failure of so many. They are pushed around by their moods, and their moods are pushed around by circumstances of life. They have reneged on personal responsibility by surrendering control of their moods to uncontrollable forces. Now the tail wags the dog. Behavioral patterns are determined by sets of circumstances rather than by personal choices. Happiness is dependent on happenings.

When our four-year-old daughter developed a little habit of overreacting to negative situations, I explained that there was "something" somewhere inside her that would rise up and make her act like she really did not want to act. Attempting to disassociate her identity from that something within, I suggested that she not let that nasty something boss her around like that. A few days later while in a crabby mood, she suddenly caught herself. Her face brightened up as she exclaimed, "Okay, dumb dumb. Sit down in there and be quiet."

I heard her with my own ears. I saw her exchange those horns for a halo. I was so sure she had the problem whipped, and that my cherub would now be her true angelic self that her kind of dad so richly deserved.

A couple of weeks later the halo faded and she was behaving again in quite a subcivilized way. It was both a blow to my teaching method and a reflection on the Murphree clan. I said, "Uh oh, girl; what are you going to do about that something inside that's bossing you around?" To which she immediately reacted, "Okay, dumb dumb in there, rise up and get worse!"

So we allow that "something" to push-button-control us. We even seem happy to relinquish authority over ourselves, and are content to be robots.

There are two very basic needs that require a vital relationship with God. The one is purely emotional, and the second, while affecting the emotions indirectly, is primarily ethical in nature.

It should be understood, however, that there are emotional problems resulting from biochemical imbalances, the physical condition of one's nerves, and other somatic disturbances—which a relationship with God is not expected to repair suddenly. There are preconditioned personality patterns and unresolved unconscious conflicts for which a relationship with God is not automatically curative. Certainly there is no Christian claim that a psychotic or a psychopath needs nothing more than a feeling of acceptance by God.

These limitations, however, do not negate what a relationship with God can do for those who are serious about gaining control of their moods.

An Inner Climate of Spirit

The first personality need that is met when a person relates to God is emotional. Ordinarily, emotions are dormant until activated by something to which they can respond. I may have the capacity to love without having an object for my love, but having the capacity to love is different from loving. Emotional activity is by nature either a response or a reaction. Even when emotion is initiated, it is the person who initiates the emotion, not the emotion initiating itself.

Left alone, emotions are expected to respond positively

to those situations (or persons, or things) that elicit
positive response, and negatively to those that elicit
negative response. A young dating couple knows very
little about each other until each sees the other in
difficult situations. They can be loving and happy and
considerate without much effort in the dating relationship.

What God provides for His close friends is an inner
climate of spirit to which the emotions can respond
when life situations would otherwise evoke negative
reaction. Appropriating divine fellowship for one's own
spirit produces an ego state that can activate the emotions for positive response. On the one hand there re-
mains the nasty temper or the pouting disposition. But
on the other hand there is an inner spiritual resource to
which a person can switch his emotions. There is an
inner nucleus of relaxation about the direction and
destiny of life, a relaxation that can overshadow the
frustrations of the situation at hand. There is "something
different" that cannot be known by the person who
knows God only remotely.

The mental switch can be flipped from inner tension
to inner relaxation. The Christian has been given something positive to which the emotions can respond—
forgiveness when we feel guilt, God's love for us when
we feel lonely or hostile, a bright future when the present
seems dark, a connection with something permanent
when we feel detached from solidness in the world.
When circumstances are on overload, the circuit breaker
can be thrown. Inside, the light of Christ can be flipped
on.

Former Los Angeles Police Chief Edward M. Davis
said, "I can look at a face and generally tell you if that
person has come to Christ. There's something different
when . . . you've accepted Jesus Christ as your Savior.

Something special happens to you. Your countenance lights up."[1]

Another way to say what I have said is this. Dedicated Christians have undergirding support for their emotions when they are in situations that would otherwise allow their emotions to bottom out. The Scripture says, "The joy of the Lord is your strength" (Neh. 8:10, RSV). There is a reason to be happy when no reason outside Christ can be found. While a Christian still feels the downward pull, he also feels the buoyancy, the upward lift. The Christian has "meat to eat that ye know not of" (John 4:32). The presence of Christ is emotionally supportive.

Flipping the Switch

What disturbs me, however, is the popular tendency to expect God's active work in the human personality to be primarily emotional rather than ethical. There is an element of emotion involved, but Christian conversion at bottom is ethical in nature. It is a conversion of our values.

With all the emotional support and security that God gives, it is still the choice of the person to respond emotionally to that support. Someone has to decide to flip the switch. That choice is a moral choice because it is the right thing to do. Mastering one's moods is a moral imperative, unless, of course, the emotions are beyond control. To relinquish emotional control is to abandon moral responsibility. All the emotional help God gives is futile unless we are willing to use that help in governing and regulating our moods.

[1]Quoted in The [Wilmore, Ky.] Herald, January, 1978, p. 10.

Notwithstanding my points of disagreement with Transactional Analysis and Realty Therapy, these systems have returned to the patient personal responsibility for improvement—a responsibility that is consistent with the Christian approach.

To be normal human beings in society, our emotions have to be structured by certain practical guidelines and social mores. This emotional structure determines what kind of personality one has and how he relates to his community. There are also ethical structures for the emotions that are needed to control one's moods.

God does not, however, merely give emotional help and leave us ethically on our own. He actually imparts the moral strength necessary to make the emotional help practical. The moral choice is still ours, but the moral strength for that choice is divinely provided.

This is a Christian claim that may not be understood by a person outside the Christian system. But so many of us within the system have experienced inner moral bracing, a new character fortitude, an inner deposit of ethical courage by which we have been able to transcend our former lives and live beyond our former strength. Whether it is an added supply of moral power given directly or the unleashing of unused power already given by God to every person, I am not prepared to argue. I rather think it is both.

The God-given emotional support would be all but useless apart from the God-given ethical power to appropriate and utilize that emotional help. The ethical is therefore just as indispensable as the emotional. With God's help, our emotional moods can be ethically mastered.

In living a life open to the presence of God we have everything required to shake out of crabbiness and develop personality patterns of happiness. This happiness is therapeutic, like a detergent released in the "blood stream" of the personality.

One man said he felt as if God had dropped an alka-seltzer tablet in his heart, and he was bubbling to the brim!

13
Pleasure and the Emotions

"Yeah, I know about the peace of mind and all that." Barry shrugged his teenage shoulders, threw a momentary glance at me and then dropped his eyes to the walk. "But it's not worth being a Christian for. I've gotta get out and have my pleasure while I'm young."

I grabbed his shoulder to make my point, and replied, "Man, you don't know what pleasure is till you get on deck with God!"

Of course, I was right—and of course, he was right. We were talking about two entirely different kinds of pleasure. Peace and pleasure are not mutually exclusive if it is the right kind of pleasure—otherwise they do not belong together.

The Analysis of Pleasure

The seventeenth-century philosopher John Locke wrote that pleasure only exists in contrast to pain and is only experienced as the sensation of going from pain to less pain. The word *pain* here is defined so broadly as to include any kind of inconvenience or discomfort, including ungratified desire.

If you will analyze every kind of pleasure known to any

85

human being, I think you find this common ingredient. Peace may be the state of having had desire satisfied, but pleasure is the process of having the desire gratified.

The obvious illustrations that come to mind are the experiences of having sex and eating food. You derive no pleasure at all from either unless you have an appetite. The pleasure is in the process of going from desire to less desire. The same is true in the pleasure a parent experiences in watching a son or daughter perform well or live right or make good. The pleasure is in the process of having the anxiety of desire alleviated. Acquiring knowledge is pure pleasure for the curious mind; working is pleasure for those who want to work; classical music is sheer pleasure for those with a musical appetite.

Emotional Complications

Some have misidentified pleasure in general with the particular kind of pleasure that is morally dubious for a child of God. But the Judeo-Christian Scriptures do not teach that pleasure is implicitly bad. The Stoics believed pleasure is inherently evil and the hedonists regard pleasure as the highest good. The Christian is somewhere between these two extremes. Pleasure is not a high priority, but it is a worthy experience to be enjoyed.

The problem with many kinds of pleasure is that the pleasure is usually short-lived. As soon as the desire is satisfied, the pleasure ceases to exist. In his *Tam o'Shanter* Robert Burns writes:

> But pleasures are like poppies spread;
> You seize the flower, its bloom is shed;
> Or like the snow falls in the river,
> A moment white—then melts forever.

The problem is complicated when the pleasure becomes so intense that the emotions cannot cope with the letdown. Intense sensation conditions human emotions for depression when the sensation is ended.

The intensity of the pleasure is obviously proportionate to the intensity of the desire. Being a finer-tuned "substance" with greater desires than the body, the mind is capable of more intense pleasure than the body. This is one reason the emotions have no problem with the aftermath of a good dinner or a sex experience, but they sometimes cannot handle the loss of a friend.

Similarly, the human spirit is even more refined than the mind—with higher potential, greater capacities and stronger desires. Being made for God, one's spirit has strong desires for love, beauty, truth, goodness and transcendent godlike qualities. These desires are often unrecognized because we become preoccupied with empirical senses that sometimes overshadow spiritual desires. But they keep erupting with a force that cannot be ignored.

Because of the strength of these spiritual desires, the human spirit has greater capacity for pleasure than either the mind or the body. (Of course, both spiritual and physical pleasures are perceived through the mind.) And this is where we find man's capacity for heaven—in his capacity for the transcendent pleasure of spirit. This is true whether the heaven be experienced in this present existence or in eternity.

Here also we discover man's capacity for hell, whether it be experienced in this life or in the life to come. This capacity is seen in the intensity of his desires for love, beauty, goodness and God. When these highest and holiest desires are ungratified, they become unbearably frustrating, pure pain, unmitigated hell. Hell is the deprivation of the very highest for which one's spirit has been made, and the frustrating desire that results from the deprivation.

Since the pleasure of spirit can be greater than either that of mind or body, we would expect the aftermath of spiritual pleasure to be severe depression. But we do not find this to be the case at all. Rather, pleasure of spirit seems to prevent emotional vulnerability to the letdown that often accompanies other pleasure. Gratification of spiritual desire produces a quality of pleasure that diminishes the need for other kinds of pleasure. It sustains the emotions.

Hooked on God

One reason for this is the continuation of spiritual pleasure. Different from many other desires, spiritual appetite is not lost by use. The desire is not eliminated by gratification.

You can eat so much banana pudding that the very thought of it becomes distasteful. You can watch New Year's Day bowl games until you are tired of football. You can overindulge in sex until you want to think of anything else. You can so tire of vacation that you wish to be home.

But something quite the contrary happens when you "indulge" spiritual desires. The more beauty you behold, the greater your capacity to enjoy more beauty. The more goodness you experience, the more of it you want. The more love you have, the more love you want to have. The closer to God you get, the closer to God you want to be. You cannot be filled with so much God that you want no more of Him. The more you taste the personality of Christ the more delicious it becomes. God is habit-forming—you get hooked on Him! The heaven in your heart may become a pool of pure liquid pleasure.

The enigma is this. Gratifying spiritual desires intensifies those desires. Gratification and intensification continue forever, producing eternal pleasure—because God is inexhaustible. There is never the emotional letdown.

An Important Distinction

Now we are talking about two things. We need to distinguish between the emotion's desire for pleasure and the desires for those experiences to which the pleasure is purely incidential.

The emotions can be hooked on pleasure. Excessive pleasure becomes obsessive. It grips us and posseses us until our emotions require it. The danger is at this very point. Lesser desires of life are so diminished by gratification that they lose their capacity to produce pleasure. But the pleasure-hooked emotions require pleasure to feed the habit. Consequently there is a greater drive and more indulgence in order to milk out of what desires are left what pleasures they can still produce. This further reduces the desires and diminishes one's capacity for pleasure. Having been hooked on pleasure, the emotions are left without a source for pleasure. Desires have been exploited and prostituted. Emotions are left hanging. The withdrawal pains are devastating.

It does not happen because we have too much pleasure, but because we have too little of the right kind of pleasure. This drives us to have too much of the wrong kind. We settle for cheap thrills and pleasure-spins that fry our emotions and dry out our desires for everything but pleasure. All the while our spirits are hurting for the pleasure for which they are made.

Please! Let no one infer that the spirit of man is made *primarily* for pleasure, nor that pleasure will be the primary ingredient of heaven. The spirit of man does not desire pleasure, but it is structured to enjoy pleasure. It desires purpose, beauty, meaning, truth, goodness, divine fellowship. Pleasure is a byproduct of having these desires gratified. The emotions are equipped to experience the pleasure derived from this gratification.

Now back to my conversation with Barry on the sidewalk. He was giving priority to his physical desires, and in so doing Barry was betraying his own emotions. His feelings all the while were being set up for a great fall. They were being conditioned for a pleasure that could not be sustained. His emotions were being jeopardized by the pleasure habit. They were not being fulfilled by the kind of pleasure that can be sustained.

What I said to him was true. The lower level pleasures barely qualify to be called pleasure in light of the kind of pleasure God has created our spirits to enjoy. "You don't know what pleasure is till you get on deck with God!"

14
Inner Conflict and Peace

The Alabama sunset had never been more brilliant. Gold shafts of rarefied light shot up from behind Cheaha Mountain in majestic splendor. High above the crest, fluffy puffs of pink cotton clouds modulated the gold and reflected a crimson hue across the valley.

I was on my dad's farm, a young teen-ager. Awe-stricken by the breathtaking beauty, I lingered long absorbing the grandeur and bathing my soul in the tranquillity.

But after several minutes I suddenly began to recoil inwardly. Though I could not understand just why, exposure to the calm beauty was creating some kind of inner conflict. The rude awakening came as an ugly surprise. The contradiction was puzzling. The serenity seemed to be producing clashing discords in my spirit. Somehow I could feel nothing within me that would blend with the refinement of the sunset.

A few years later I gained an inner sense of assurance of my personal relationship with God through Jesus Christ. The assurance was characterized by a sense of acceptance and forgiveness, and it was accompanied by higher ideals, new purposes and an expanded quality of life.

At the time I had all but forgotten the miserably beautiful sunset experience. Several weeks later, however, it all came back to me as I watched another gorgeous sunset, this one like the other, resplendent with color. Quite unexpectedly something totally different began happening inside. It has never been my practice to place any priority on the analyses of my own feelings, but this rang with so much clarity that it was unavoidable. Strange music was resounding inside me, music that seemed to originate beyond the sunset. My soul was singing. It blended so harmoniously with the aesthetic. Not that I was so beautiful in my heart, but there were no clashing discords. The conflict was gone. There was harmony, tranquillity, peace.

Emotions Need a Retreat

Peace is not an emotion, but rather it is a state or condition of mind or emotions. There may be, however, emotion associated with the condition of peace. As in my case watching the sunset, inward peace produced a joy that was akin to celestial music. Conversely, those who become conditioned to conflict can become emotionally bored with no conflict at all. Either way, peace is felt in contrast to the conflict. In time, the emotion associated with the peace will subside—though the condition of peace may remain.

This is precisely what the emotions need. They need to be thrown in neutral for a period. They need rest and relaxation. They need to settle back, to shake the habit of excessive joy or sorrow, to become unhooked for awhile. They need to recover from overuse.

Without this retreat, emotions can become thin, frayed and threadbare. Too much strain and stress can wear them out. Just as the body needs a daily recovery and replenishing period that we call sleep, the emotions need sanctuary from continuous conflict.

This emotional refuge is provided in a personal relationship with God. In order to understand how this works, we need to see two sources of conflict, both of which produce inner agitation and turmoil.

Outside Conflicts

First, there is the conflict between man and his environment, social as well as physical. Tensions arise between husband and wife, parent and child, employer and employee. The stock market drops, threatening your investment. Something you said was misinterpreted, and a misunderstanding develops between you and your neighbor. Your limited salary or job insecurity has caused more anxieties than even your wife knows about.

These outside disturbances make you uptight. Then the tension mounts until little annoyances are blown up to major crises. The way your spouse squeezes the toothpaste tube bugs you. Voice tones and facial expressions get under your skin and irritate you.

Chances are, this situation escalated in the beginning because there was no inward emotional asylum for the feelings. There was no deposit of divine presense to dissolve the little irritations as they came up. The emotions had no retreat center. They had no escape valve—no spiritual Companion to unload their feelings on. The emotions had to collect and hold the stress and strain until the load got too heavy.

A meaningful relationship with God becomes a fallout shelter. It is like a storm cellar. The emotions need to come in out of the storm. The psalmist seemed to be alluding to an emotional nest when he sang, "He will cover you with his pinions, and under his wings you will find refuge . . . You will not fear the terror of the night, nor the arrow that flies by day . . . Because you have made the Lord your refuge, the Most High your habitation . . ." (Psalm 91:4, 5, 9, RSV).

The emotional support of companionship with God is like a protective coating for the emotions. A storm door guards the emotional home. The occupant can have a repose that is unaffected by the stock market, the weather forecast or his daily horoscope.

To change the illustration, God can be like a thermostat to your emotions. The human body has an internal regulator that keeps the bodily temperature the same regardless of temperature changes on the outside. A body becomes feverish not when something goes wrong on the outside, but when something fouls up on the inside. Relating to God keeps the emotions well when nothing goes well on the outside. Where there is outside disturbance the emotions can turn to an inner regulator for composure. When there is outside conflict there is an inner haven.

This is not to say there will be peace automatically. But when outside pressures are at their worst, there is an inner shelter to which we can resort—if the relationship with God is intact. We have staked our lives in Christ on values that are unshakable and conditions that are not turbulent. At the center we can be relaxed, like the calm eye of a hurricane while violent wind is swirling all around. Companionship with God provides the emotional resources and support for each of us to become a practitioner of peace.

A Peacetime Economy

We would expect outside disturbances to produce inner emotional conflict. But when I viewed the sunset as an early youth, it was outside calm and beauty, not outside turbulance, that disturbed my spirit and produced inner conflict.

This illustrates the second source of conflict—one that is easily overlooked by the counselor who is purely humanistic in his outlook. It is not the tension between man and his environment, but the conflict between man and God. It is the disharmony within one's spirit between what he is and what he was intended to be, between what his spirit has and the godlike qualities it was created to have. It is the tension between feelings of ugliness and the capacity for beauty, a tension between egotism and the goodness and selflessness for which he has been made. The human spirit is not at home in its feelings of self-centeredness, guilt, ugliness and vanity.

Over fifteen centuries ago Augustine expressed it succinctly in *The City of God:* "O Lord. Thou hast made us for Thyself, and we are restless until we find our rest in Thee."

Created for divine purposes, for holy impulses, for higher values, for transcendent meaning and fellowship with God, there can never be inward harmony and personality integration with unholy impulses, meaninglessness, purposelessness and unworthy values. It is like a woman with a Ph.D. in English literature who expects compatability of interests in a marriage with a high-school dropout. It is like an M.D. who settles for a job pumping gasoline. He is bored, ill-at-ease, dissatisfied.

Since our spirits are made for more than they can ever have without God, there is uneasiness, spiritual dissatisfaction, inward turmoil, no peace. We feel like strangers to ourselves, make-believe characters rather than authentic persons. Without God we are suffering from a deficit of spirit, a collapse of our spiritual economy, without resources to prevent spiritual bankruptcy. Deep within, our spirits remain anxious and apprehensive, fearful and frustrated, still restless and still searching. The quest will go on until the spirit finds its native habitat in God.

A relationship with God opens up a new world of spiritual reality, one which provides the wealth to satisfy your poverty-stricken spirit. It creates a peacetime economy in your soul. A sense of settledness will dissolve the tensions and turmoil between you and God, and give you a security in a society that may remain restless and insecure. The conflict of spirit is *resolved* in peace *with* God, and the conflict between you and your environment is *dissolved* in the peace *of* God.

15
Love and . . .

A preschool-age lad in Kentucky had a knack for using big words. His dad was a college professor, and the boy would pick up these multisyllable terms and spit them out, sometimes appropriately but more often inappropriately. One afternoon he was overheard saying to a three-year-old neighbor girl, "I love you." There was an awkward pause, and then he asked, "Do you reciprocate?"

Initiated and Reciprocal

Humor aside, the lad was expressing a clear distinction between two kinds of love that is often fuzzy. "I love you" is initiated love. "Do you reciprocate?" refers to reciprocal or responsive love.

The blurring of this distinction by society in general has created a confusing problem. Is love to be thought of in moral terms or purely emotional ones? And how can love be both moral and emotional at the same time?

According to Jesus, all moral obligations are wrapped up in the commandment to love (Matt. 22:35-40). We hear exhortations from all quarters to love, as if loving is an option that can be chosen or rejected.

Yet "I don't love you anymore" is considered a virtuous, "honest" expression—as if a person is helpless to do anything about it. "She doesn't turn me on," "The flame has died," "He doesn't do anything for me," "I don't feel any sparks"—these declarations assume that a person is the helpless victim of something that grabs him in the chest.

Loving on this assumption is purely emotional with no moral responsibility. Extramarital relationships are justified because "I couldn't help it; I fell in love with him." This assumes a person is not responsible for his actions when he is motivated by emotion. Moral responsibility ends where emotion begins. Emotional feeling is a monster we must serve without even an inclination toward resistance. Rather than acting either appropriately or inappropriately, we are simply being acted upon, leaving us neither praiseworthy nor deserving of blame.

On the same grounds some behaviorists have asserted that those who have hostilities, violent tempers and abusive attitudes are not to be condemned, because they are driven by an emotional force that is beyond their ability to counter.

If love is an emotion for which we are not responsible, it is foolish to speak of love in moral terms. Oughtness and ought-notness are irrelevant notions. Jesus' commandment to love is contradictory. We are not supposed to have the foggiest idea about how we can go about choosing to love.

If I can be allowed a loose characterization, initiated love is moral in nature and reciprocal love is basically emotional. Initiated love at bottom is the choice to love even when there is no emotional motive involved. Reciprocal love, on the other hand, does include a moral element, in that a person is responsible for choosing to respond or not to respond, but the motive at bottom is emotional.

Is Love an Emotion?

I even question whether a love that is emotionally motivated exclusively should even be considered love at all. The "feeling" of love is an emotion, but love is fundamentally something other. It is a favorable disposition toward someone rather than a favorable emotion toward that someone. I do not intend to suggest that a favorable disposition alone is necessarily love. In order for a favorable disposition to be equated with love, the definitions for both words of the phrase must be loaded with their heaviest cargo—a solid disposition of extreme favor. In any case, the point is that love stripped of its extras is a certain disposition toward someone rather than a certain emotion.

If love is a favorable disposition, loving then is the expression of that disposition. The feeling is merely the emotion tied to the disposition. Emotion is useful in making the loving easier, but it is not standard equipment. I will make a concession to popular opinion by allowing the emotionally motivated disposition to be called love—provided we distinguish it as reciprocal rather than initiated love.

Reciprocal love is self-centered; initiated love is other-centered. The first is primarily conscious of one's own feelings—the feeling of being loved, feeling flattered by being loved, or feeling the security of being loved. The second is conscious of the other person's desires, needs, hurts and happiness.

Reciprocal love is demanding; it is based on receiving the recognition, the distinction, the flattery of initiated love. Initiated love is based on giving, and it functions without reciprocation. It takes chances, runs risks and makes great sacrifice. It is tough and tenacious, and reaches out without counting the cost. It is unconditional, has no price tag, and takes its own losses. Initiated love is its own security.

Reciprocal love comes easily, almost helplessly. "I fell for him. I couldn't help it." "In his arms I was as helpless as a child." The emotional motivation makes reciprocal love almost involuntary. But it is vaporous and empty, unchosen and void of initiative.

Love and Romance

This is the one biggest problem with American marriages today—they are built on emotion rather than choice. Romantic love is initiated by personal appeal, good looks or common emotional needs rather than by a moral choice to love in the practical nitty-gritty of life. It requires a romantic setting—moonlight, candles, or a sunset on the beach. When these stage props are gone, reciprocal love loses its emotional motivation. There is nothing to fall back on.

Married couples do not live in perpetual romantic settings. They have to share toothpaste and hand towels, and see wrinkles and pimples. Often they even have to change diapers. The mystique of romantic love lets them down. Marital relationships become meaningful only when they are personally initiated by voluntary choice.

In "The Life of Father Damien," Robert Louis Stevenson tells of the poor Belgian priest who gave his life to help the lepers on the island of Molokai and who himself died of the disease. "Damien went there," says Stevenson, "and shut . . . with his own hand the door of his own sepulcher . . . and slept that first night under a tree with his rotting brethren, alone with pestilence, and looking forward . . . to a lifetime of dressing sores." That is initiated love, chosen, and unaltered by circumstance. The lover is victimized not by emotions, but only by one's own choice to love.

In our society today we have a great shortage of initiated love, and this is creating monumental problems. A person who is deprived of love is not equipped to initiate love. We first learn to love by being loved. The very first love a child feels toward a parent is reciprocal rather than initiated. Only after a child has had these lavish experiences of reciprocal love is he equipped to initiate love. It may sound like a tautology, but the reason for the shortage of initiated love is a shortage of initiated love. Because we require love somewhere along the way to get started loving, a love deficit produces an even greater love deficit. If the process is to be reversed, initiated love must break in.

God's Initiated Love

This is where God comes in. Expressed theologically in the incarnation, God chose to break in on our greed-ridden, hate-laden world with a daring love that was so costly it took Him to a cross. At that cross He was exposing everyone of us to the most courageous love we have ever known. He was breaking in on our deprived spirits with an initiated love that had no limits, asked no questions and required no response. "God shows his love for us in that while we were yet sinners Christ died for us" (Rom. 5:8, RSV).

God does not love us because of what we are, but because of what He is. Therefore He does not quit loving us because of what we are not. His love is not drawn out by our goodness; it is poured out from His goodness. It is morally motivated rather than emotionally motivated.

He loves us no more because we are lovable and no less because we are unlovely—no more because we are good and no less because we are bad. He loves me in spite of me! He loves you in spite of you!

It is the kind of love our emotions can respond to. It provides us with distinction, security, recognition beyond the highest human scale. His love is beautiful against the ugly backdrop of Calvary. It is appealing. It wins my heart. Everything within me wants to reciprocate. I am given an emotional motive to love Him in return.

The commandment Jesus called "the first and great commandment"—Thou shalt love the Lord thy God—at first sight looks harsh and demanding. It sounds as if God expects from us an initiated love that we are not morally equipped to give. The second commandment—Thou shalt love thy neighbor—seems equally difficult. How can I love a neighbor who cares not a snap for me? Deprived of love and with no emotional motive, my heart cannot be expected to initiate a love toward those who are neither lovable nor deserving.

In light of the overtures of Calvary-love, however, we see the commandments in a radically different focus. It breaks in on us like a flash of brilliance that reciprocal love is what the first commandment requires, not initiated love at all. Though we may be ill-equipped morally to initiate a love for God, we are given an emotional motive that makes it easy. "We love him, because he first loved us" (I John 4:19). He only asks us to reciprocate His love that is in fact all but irresistible. Even the most morally destitute character in the world can respond. It seems so easy. But it is all He asks—at the start.

16
. . . Hostilities

Then comes the second commandment. Yes, I can love God—that's no problem. But please don't ask me to love my neighbor. Not *my* neighbor. That is a different story. That's something I didn't bargain for when I responded to God's love. To love my neighbor is just too much.

You see, you just don't know what Chuck said about me. He lies. He is always riding me about something. He gets in my hair. He and I have a personality clash. That Chuck really has an annoying way about him. I don't need his friendship anyhow—I'm better off without it. Besides, he has an arrogant air that turns me off.

Still, there's that second commandment. I can try to be evasive. I may try to hedge and duck it, and make my excuses sound plausible. But the commandment stands. I must love Chuck.

When Jesus said, "Thou shalt love thy neighbor," He obviously was not speaking of reciprocal love. The first commandment is reciprocal, with an emotional motive to love God. But the second requires an initiated love that often includes no emotional motive at all. God first asked us only to reciprocate His love. Now He asks us to prove it by initiating love for others.

It is a moral obligation to be favorably disposed toward those who have no appeal and who have nothing to offer in return. It is a commandment to give love without requiring reciprocation, even to be vulnerable to having our love rejected. It is a practical thing we are commanded to do—to love when there is no sentiment, to care when there is no reward, to act with concern when the action endangers our self-interests. God requires a dangerous self-abandonment, preferring others to ourselves, turning the other cheek and going the second mile.

It sounds so hard. The last time I tried it I got knocked flat on my back. It was such an embarrassing position. I had to grin and bear it, to get up and walk again. My emotions had trouble shaking the rebuff. It took me days to re-collect my cool. I feel I just cannot chance it again. But the commandment has not been revoked. I have got to love Chuck.

Equipped to Love

At this very point comes another brilliant flash of enlightenment. It is so obvious we wonder how we ever could have missed it. Again we are amazed at the way human psychology, moral ethics and Christian theology fit together as interlocking pieces.

God's initiated love for us not only makes reciprocal love toward Him come easily. It actually equips us to initiate love toward others. We are no longer deprived of love. His love provides the distinction and security that we need to enable us to love without requiring the security of response. Feeling the emotional support of His love, we can choose to love with a moral motive without demanding an emotional motive. Having learned to reciprocate love, we are in a position to initiate love. The greatest problem in loving a neighbor is resolved in loving God.

It is like a piece of iron being rubbed against a magnet. The iron in turn becomes magnetic. Our hearts may have been as cold and hard as iron. But they become magnetized by His magnetism. The magnetic forces of love reaching out from His heart pulled us to Himself. Not only did our iron hearts respond to His magnetic love, but that love created a magnetic field around *us*. Now there flows out from our hearts magnetic forces of love. His initiated magnetism toward us has equipped us with initiating magnetism toward others. "If God so loved us, we also ought to love one another" (I John 4:11, RSV).

Not only does loving God condition us to love our neighbor; God's initial love for us actually deposits an *emotional* motive to love others. So after all my complaining about how difficult it is to love Chuck, I discover that being kindly disposed toward him is not mere initiated love toward him after all. There is an element of reciprocation involved. It is not a reciprocation of Chuck's love, since he cares not a whit for me. My initiated love toward him is a part of my reciprocal love toward God.

Have you ever noticed what happens to a young man when he is in love with a young woman? He begins to take an interest in her likes and dislikes, to be charmed by the things that are charming to her, to give attention to those things that interest her. Her family becomes sort of special to him. Rather than demanding that she walk into his world, he walks into hers. She responds by becoming a part of his. Her world becomes his and his world becomes hers. He takes an interest in Beethoven

and she gets interested in the Dallas Cowboys. He pats
her dog and picks on her kid brother. He even develops a
fixation on her brand of cologne.

This is sort of what happens when we love God—that
is, when we really love God. We *want* to love what God
loves. We take an interest in God's interests. God has
walked into our world with initiated love. Now we walk
into God's world with responsive love. We have an
emotional motive for loving all people everywhere. God
loves them, and we love God. To complete the equation,
we love them too. There is still the moral motive, but
there is also the motive of emotional desire. My favorable
attitude toward Chuck is initiated toward him, but it is
also a part of my larger reciprocal love toward God.
Without God's love I might never be able to love Chuck.
With God's love, it is easier than I had originally supposed.

Social Implications

To obey the second commandment means two things.
First, it means to concern ourselves with those who have
not necessarily wronged us but who have nothing to offer
us in return. Their well-being is not included in our
self-interests: the world hunger problem, prison conditions, the plight of ethnic minorities, the diseased and
suffering, those who are grief-stricken, lonely and hurting
for love. Jesus included our willingness to help the needy
as a part of our reciprocal love for Him, and our refusal to
do so as our rejection of Him. He was speaking of the
poor, the imprisoned, the lonely and the hungry when He
said, "Verily I say unto you, Inasmuch as ye have done it
unto one of the least of these my brethren, ye have done
it unto me . . . Inasmuch as ye did it not to one of the
least of these, ye did it not to me" (Matt. 25:40, 45). By

identifying with the oppressed and the dispossessed, Jesus installed an emotional motive to help us love those who are unloved and unwanted. It is a part of our reciprocal love for Him.

Second, obedience to the second commandment means an attitude of forgiveness toward every Chuck that has abused us in any way. We are to forgive "seventy times seven" times (Matt. 18:22, RSV).

Here we find God's psychological remedy for the most devastating, debilitating attitude ever known—hostility. The human personality has not been made for animosity. We can stand up under the pressure of being hated more easily than under the pressure of hating. Less damage is done to the one hated than to the one doing the hating. Hostility stings the hater, tantalizes and torments him incessantly. Unresolved hostilities filter down deep and erupt in the form of distorted emotional patterns, mental imbalance or even physical disorders.

God's psychological remedy begins with His initiated love—the perfect example of the forgiveness we are expected to initiate toward those who have offended us. Our offenses were grievous to the point of causing His death on the cross. Yet His love followed us with forgiveness every step of the way. Only after He has forgiven us of our death-causing crimes against Him does He ask us to forgive those He loves who have offended us—for His sake, as a part of our responsive love toward Him. An emotional motive is thus established that is hard for us to reject.

Equipped with both an additional emotional motive to love others and an inexhaustible supply of divine favor giving us security and emotional support, we reciprocate His love by loving our neighbor. His love is emotionally cleansing. Festering hostilities are dissolved. Damaged emotions are healed because selfish motives are cleansed. We have a workable way to get ourselves off the hate hook. The rats that have been gnawing at our personalities are destroyed; the cockroaches are exterminated.

The ethical and the emotional embrace each other. Moral obligations are psychologically possible. And by keeping these two greatest commandments we qualify for living as a part of the high order of the Kingdom of God.

17
Worship

Speaking of the person who experiences worship in its most exalted form, Wordsworth said in *The Excursion:*

> In such an hour
> Of visitation from the living God . . .
> No thanks he breathed, he proffered no request;
> Rapt into still communion that transcends
> The imperfect offices of prayer and praise . . .

Any consideration of how human emotions relate to God would be glaringly incomplete without pondering at least in passing the experience of worship. For worship is the highest, purest, most selfless and exalted activity ever to engross the emotions.

In *The Hope of a New World* William Temple says: "To worship is to quicken the conscience by the holiness of God, to feed the mind with the truth of God, to purge the imagination by the beauty of God, to open the heart to the love of God, to devote the will to the purpose of God."[1]

---

[1] William Temple, *The Hope of a New World* (New York: Arno Press, 1940).

A Clashing Contrast

Earlier I detailed a number of man-related maxims emerging from the religious teaching of divine creation. At least two of these maxims converge at the point of worship and help us understand what is meant by Christian worship and why it is so emotionally necessary for humankind.

First, to be created by God means we have a derived existence, are dependent rather than independent, and therefore are limited and finite. This is all very well; it can all be said of animal or vegetable life. The finiteness of our existence, however, is complicated by the second maxim. We are not only created by God—we are created for God. This means we are spiritual creatures, and our spirits are transcendent. Being created for God, we are created for ultimateness, leaving us with both a desire for that which is ultimate and a capacity to conceptualize the idea of the ultimate.

With finite existence and transcendent spirits, we are in a position to observe both our own finiteness and the ultimateness that is beyond us. At times our spatial and temporal limitations seem to suffocate our spirits. We feel as if we occupy a position that cannot adequately accommodate our potential. So emotionally we keep standing on tiptoe, peering beyond, trying to get a peek over the wall.

It is in this clashing contrast that worship is born—in the contrast between what man sees himself to be and what he perceives beyond him to be. One of the key words is *mystery*. Worship is the humble—repeat, *humble*—exploration of that which is awesomely beyond. Worship is wonder and marvel at the mysterious quality of that which is adored. It is openness and responsiveness to the unknown that is vaguely recognized and only broadly perceived. It includes admiration and reverence for that something rare, excellent and sublime.

Worship connotes an element of awe, even a passion of wonder. So much so that the emotions in genuine worshiping experiences are all but lost to all other feelings. In *The Religion of a Literary Man* (1894), English author Richard Le Gallienne writes, "Wherever we have the sense of wonder, . . . we have one of the germs of that spiritual insight which sees the world . . . bathed in that strange light."

In the experience of worship a person often has a strange combination of opposing feelings. On the one hand he feels the contrast between himself and the object of his worship. On the other hand, driven by his transcendent spirit, he feels an identification with that which he worships. There is the urge to identify beyond oneself. So while feeling his individual separateness he also feels a spiritual unity, a sense of oneness with that which he considers worthy of worship.

We see this unusual combination of feelings regardless of what one chooses to worship—whether God, or political figures, show biz personalities, or even one's own dad. The person feels inferior to the worship object, but in worshiping he feels an identity with the object. By worshiping he is able to identify beyond himself.

Even when a person worships himself, he ordinarily worships something about himself that he wants to feel an identity with. It may be his good looks, the muscular build of his body, special skills, professional expertise or social adroitness. Whatever, he differentiates between what he is and what he wants to be, or between what he is afraid he is and what he hopes he is. The distinction is there and it means unexplored mysteries. In identifying with that something else, in self-worship the person attempts to shift his image of himself.

Choosing a God

Here a grave danger is lurking or a great good is in the offing—determined by what I choose to worship. My spirit is made for God. But if I refuse to worship God, my worship-prone spirit will drive me to worship something else. Whatever it may be, it will have to be something less than God. This means I am identifying with something less than I have been made to identify with, and I am settling for something short of my potential. Someone said, "When you bow the knee to a god that is smaller than the true God, you become smaller than a true human."

Worshiping a god that is too small has frightening implications. It means my spirit-progress is arrested and my growth is impeded. My emotions have to settle for a limited joy, well below their potential for spiritual joy. The transcendent inclinations of my spirit are inhibited. I can never rise above the object of my worship.

Only God is big enough, beautiful, good and mysterious enough for a spirit like yours and mine. Everything else is finite, and finiteness is inadequate for transcendent spirits. When it is explored it loses its mystery, and loses its appeal for worship.

After a young woman has been married a few months, she begins to unpack her spouse's personality. She understands him. He loses the appeal of his mystery.

A small boy idolizes his dad—until the lad becomes a teen-ager. Then he understands his father's inclinations, motivations and prejudices. He can read his dad like an open book. What had seemed so concealed, so mysterious, so impossibly beyond him, now has been explored.

There is not left enough mystery to inspire wonder. As an object of worship the dad, in spite of his best efforts, has let his son down. The father could not help being finite. It was not his fault the son was created for divine Father rather than human father.

The simple truth is that no person is qualified to sustain worship appeal—without keeping distance to prevent exploration. We worshipers have spirits that require in a god a personality that is inexhaustible, one that can be eternally investigated and still be mysterious. This we have in God. The more we explore His personality, the greater the mystery becomes.

Emotional Benefits

Now the good that awaits those of us who make God the object of worship. First, worshiping God disentangles me from myself and liberates me from the lesser gods, the worship of which would bind me, enslave me and interrupt the pilgrimage of my spirit. Worshiping God, I identify with a Person who leads me endlessly upward. My transcendent spirit is given unlimited potential. I have identified infinitely beyond myself.

Second, while identifying my spirit with the transcendent, divine worship nevertheless defines all over again for me the limitations of my own existence. In spite of the identity, the stark contrast is always sobering. It keeps my proper position in perspective. But the identity experienced in worship makes it easy for me to live with my limitations. I can accept the finiteness of my existence when my spirit soars with transcendence.

Third, by worshiping God my emotions are given the content they need. Consistent with my transcendent spirit, my emotions are capable of the very noblest, most elevated, most sublime feelings. Devoid of worship, my emotions are below their potential, impoverished, lacking in adequate content. They resort to all kinds of substitute experiences, and I feel deceived—as if the emotions are artificial. And there is always a letdown.

Penetrating the personality of Christ is the most exalted of all experiences. In worshiping God I feel the most unselfish love, purity and blessedness. The feelings are so clean. Unworthy emotions are lost somewhere along the way of worship. My feelings are given new content. And there is no letdown. To my emotions, it is a foretaste of glory—the appetizer for the eternal banquet.

18
Eternal Life

To the players it all seemed like a bad joke.

The Kansas City Royals had worked hard and played superbly for six months. They had won 102 games during the season, more than any other team in baseball. They had reeled off sixteen consecutive wins. Now they were in the playoffs against the New York Yankees for the American League pennant. Each team had won twice in the five-game series, and this was the final game—and the last inning. The winner would go to the World Series.

It was October 9, 1977. Going into the ninth the Royals led, three to two. All they had to do was hold on *one more inning!* But for the second consecutive year they blew the lead and flunked the final. The Yankees won the game five to three.

The punch line came from Kansas City second baseman Frank White. He sat in the dressing room after the game with the rest of the team. The air they breathed was heavy with anguish. Throwing up his hands in despair, White exclaimed, "What a joke. You play hard for six months and eight innings and it all goes up in one fatal inning."[1]

What a joke!

Now I want to ask: Is life a cruel joke that is being played on the participants? Will our highest dreams all go up in one fatal, final inning? Are all our hopes and aspirations empty? Are our holiest emotions being strung along and deceived? Will the desires of our spirits only burst like bubbles and our moral and spiritual strivings mock us in the end?

Or—will our strongest spiritual desires be fulfilled, as hunger is satisfied with food and thirst is slaked with water? Will our highest dreams for love, beauty and goodness someday be fulfilled more completely than we ever dared to dream?

Will all life in its final inning add up to zero, or will it reach an appropriate destiny and a meaningful goal? One way, the emotions attached to spiritual desires are betrayed. The other way, they are satisfied. It is the difference between cosmic fatality and eternal fulfillment.

Some may think I am hung up on the notion of man's transcendent spirit. I confess to the charge. But what is so appalling is that we are *all* hung up on it emotionally. Our emotions are "plagued" with the problem. This alone does not prove there is life after death, but it does prove there ought to be. The emotions require it for their fulfillment. The spirit's capacity for the transcendent creates the emotional need for it to be fulfilled.

There are at least three ways human emotions need the kind of life after death that is taught in the Christian Scriptures.

[1]Associated Press report, *The Birmingham* [Ala.] *News*, 10 October 1977, p. 29.

A Reachable Destiny

First, we need a spiritual destiny that is adequate for the emotional requirements—a destiny that will accommodate the capacity and potential of the spirit.

We all know it is the climax of any activity that gives it meaning; it is the goal toward which the effort moves that makes the effort worthwhile. Most of our goals in life are too small and therefore without sufficient challenge. They are reached too easily and then cease to be goals. We feel the way I did when I recently finished working a jigsaw puzzle—"so what?" The goal was conquered and the challenge was lost. I felt as if the destiny did not justify the striving. There was emotional discouragement rather than fulfillment.

Those goals we have that are not too small are often too far out of reach. We condition our emotions for discouragement by setting unattainable goals. Our passions are consumed and our energy is burned up, and still the destiny is not reached. Again there is emotional discouragement.

What we need is a destiny that is continually challenging and at the same time reachable. One that is both unreached and being reached. One that is really neither attained nor unattained. For the Christian, heaven is a certainty. In that sense it is attained while it is in the process of being attained.

For the Kansas City Royals, the entire season seemed lost. The destiny was not reached. But for the New York Yankees, the goal was not adequate for the spirits of the players. They reached the destiny, but they had not yet reached their spiritual destiny. The goal was only adequate for prestige and pocketbook. It was too small for the destiny of life.

William Wordsworth wrote:

> Whether we be young or old,
> Our destiny, our being's heart and home,
> Is with infinitude, and only there;
> With hope it is, hope that can never die,
> Effort, and expectation and desire.
> And something evermore about to be.

The destiny of man's spirit is the fulfillment of his highest hopes and his holiest dreams. His emotions need the security of knowing the long quest will not have been in vain. Though unworthy dreams may explode into nightmares, short-range hopes are buried and worldly ambitions are broken, the aspirations that really matter will not be dashed in a final inning. Life is not ultimately fatal. Our emotions need this assurance. For me, I could hardly live without it.

The Security of Permanence

Not only do our emotions need a destiny for our dreams, but in an unreliable world of constant change, our emotions also need the security of permanence.

Life on earth is a one-way street, and not one of us is standing still on this street. One moment once lived can never be relived. We will never again be as young as we are this very second. These golden moments of life are slipping through our fingers and passing into history. There is no way we can capture and keep for ourselves one minute beyond one minute's time. The relationships that seemed so secure are crumbling, family members are changing their addresses, friends are dying. Our position in our social group is precarious. With every watch tick, every heartbeat, every passing moment, we are racing away from the present and into the future. What is now so present with us will soon be remote and irrecoverable. Our emotions glance backward with nostalgia, as we creep around each corner of life with uncertainty, hoping for some sort of emotional security. With all of life in a state of flux and neither the past nor the present enduring, we must attach our emotions to some kind of permanence in the future as a foundation for present emotional stability. Without it, the emotions become vulnerable to serious complications.

This was illustrated to me on a smaller scale when I was returning home after several weeks of ministering with various mission groups in Latin America. I had come to love the local people and to feel a part of their world. They had walked into my heart and captured my affection. But now I was leaving never to see them again. The experience was ugly and I was emotionally flat. The one thing that sustained me was my destiny. I was returning to my native land for permanent residence. Without this, emotionally I would have been on empty. While high over the Caribbean I recorded in my journal: "Below me are deep waters, behind are those dear people to whom I have ministered, but ahead is a star-spangled sky! And soon this big aerial room will be under the canopy of liberty and justice for all. Strange how warm I feel inside tonight."

The phrase "going home" is the most emotionally reassuring phrase in the language. While we are traveling away from the emotional support of the past, we are traveling toward a future support that is permanent. The anticipation of permanent residence sustains us in the transient circumstances of life. "And there shall be no more death, neither sorrow, nor crying, neither shall there be any more pain: for the former things are passed away" (Rev. 21:4). This may be criticized as "honey and pie in the sky bye and bye," but for those who sorrow and weep with pain and death, the future is not so irrelevant.

In a changing society with disruptive forces and fleeting moments of security, the Christian faith offers a constant. Those who gain an assurance of future life are given the emotional support for living in the present. This is so helpful and utilitarian that even a pure humanist would be hard put to deny its value.

Life Is for Keeps

Third, human emotions need assurance of eternal life. Survival desire is perhaps the most stubborn, most tenacious desire of mortals. It is sustained through the most hapless experiences, even when there is no reason to survive. A person loses everything to live for, and still he wants to live. Because man has been made to live, he wants life. The emotions are relentlessly attached to this desire.

Our emotions need the security of knowing Longfellow's lines are true:

> Life is real and life is earnest
>   And the grave is not its goal.
> 'Dust thou art, to dust returneth'
>   Was not spoken of the soul.

We need to know that life is for keeps, that we are made for eternity, that life is not a closed system.

With this survival assurance, human emotions can react more positively to fearful situations in life. If your bank account is depleted, you have a savings account in heaven. If your home burns, you have another home that is noncombustible. They can even kill you, and you will not die. What a way to live!

One of my college professors, a tremendous Christian, was sharing his faith with an unbeliever sitting next to him on an airplane. Suddenly an engine burst into flames, the plane swerved, and they were almost certain a crash was inevitable. The unbeliever was so unnerved he was almost climbing the walls of the cabin. The professor responded, "Well, goodbye, my friend. When you go down, I'll go up!"

With this kind of emotional security, we can hang loose in the world because we are attached beyond the world. Here we can roll with the punches. We can develop a lifestyle that is based on the confidence we have in Christ for eternal life. Our emotions have what they need for this kind of life in this kind of world.

Every inning is safe and secure, because the final inning will not be fatal.

19
The Divine Quest

A number of years ago I wrote a Christian novel, *The Incredible Discovery* (now out of print). While preparing the manuscript, it hit me with great force that a writer of fiction enjoys a special kind of freedom no essayist or historian ever had. I could create my own characters for the story—the kind of characters I wanted—and I had the power to make my characters say and do anything I wished. They were subject to me, they obeyed me, they could not move without me. I was their creator.

The feeling I got while writing the book was strange and unfamiliar. I wanted so much to have fellowship with my characters. For weeks I entered into their lives. I thought about them and I pondered what moves I would have them make. I got a real urge to get in that plot with them and help them work it out. And I did.

Still, it was frustrating. I could make them fellowship with one another, but they could have no fellowship with me. They became a part of my life, but I could never really become a part of theirs. I had to remain detached and aloof, because they were only characters of fiction. They were real to me, but they were not real. I knew

them, but they could never know me. I became attached
to them, but they could never feel close to me. I was
above them and beyond them. I could observe them in
detail and do with them as I pleased, but I could never
have fellowship with them.

Did God Need Man?

In this book I have dealt primarily with the human
search for God, and I have shown how man needs God
from the emotional standpoint. My focus has been
human-centered, which of course is the psychological
approach. But the Christian faith is God-centered. It
begins with what God is, and from here it sees man's
departure from God as the cause of his greatest dilemmas.

Psychology may discover man's search for God to
fulfill his deepest emotional needs. But Christian theology
teaches that God in a greater way has taken the
initiative in searching for man. This is precisely what
man needs psychologically—as he moves toward God he
needs to know God is moving toward him, that God in
fact has initiated reconciliation and fellowship. While
theology is either rejected or neglected by many of our
contemporary professional counselors, Christian theology
does in fact accommodate psychotherapy by offering
foundational support for man's deepest emotional needs.

If God created man, however, and moved courageously
to regain fellowship with man, one cannot help but
wonder why God might be up to such a project. Did He
feel as I felt while I was creating fiction? Did God
Himself have an emotional need that motivated such an
enterprise? Did He use us as pawns on His chessboard to
fulfill His basic needs? If so, does this not mean God is

incomplete within Himself, dependent rather than independent?

In order to be God at all, however, He is necessarily independent in His existence, self-contained and self-fulfilled.

We need to understand the difference between *need* and *desire*. Owing to God's nature of love, He has *desires* which extend beyond Himself. This does not violate the proposition of self-fulfillment. Christianity teaches God had near irrepressible desire for fellowship with His creatures. Because He loved, HE could not shut up His glory and majesty within Himself. He was prompted by love to share His best, even Himself, with His creatures. He got in our plot and helped us work it out. When we fouled up, He rewrote the script.

The Intended Fellowship

And God did something for us that I was not able to do for my characters of fiction. He made us capable of having meaningful fellowship with Himself, and this logically required the privilege of free moral choice. And this free choice logically required God to relinquish a power over His characters that I retained over mine—the power to do with them as I chose. Giving us freedom meant God was surrendering His freedom over us. He could no longer move us about on the stage of life at His own will. He gave up control over us so that we could enter into a voluntary, freely chosen fellowship with Him.

Instead of the intended fellowship, we used our privilege of freedom precisely to prevent that fellowship. We seized control of our own lives, crowded God out and refused to allow His fellowship. Still He would not write us off. Driven by His love, He identified with His own creatures in a way I could never identify with mine and allowed Himself to be killed on a cross by His own created characters. All the while He desired fellowship with His creatures.

In my novel, I made my characters to become Christian in the end—every one of them. I could do it, for I had not given them a choice in the matter. God is doing everything possible to make us, His characters, Christian —everything short of forcing us against our own wills. He gives the choice to us. I'm saying yes. I hope you say yes, too. The emotional fulfillment and satisfaction is beyond anything we can ever otherwise know.